my tiny
flower garden

Matt Collins

Photography by Roo Lewis

my tiny
flower garden

BEAUTIFUL BLOOMS IN SURPRISINGLY SMALL SPACES

PAVILION

First published in the United Kingdom in 2017 by
Pavilion
43 Great Ormond Street
London
WC1N 3HZ

Copyright © Pavilion Books Company Ltd 2017
Text copyright © Matt Collins 2017

ISBN 978-1-91090-473-2

A CIP catalogue record for this book is available from the British Library.

10 9 8 7 6 5 4 3 2 1

Reproduction by Mission Productions Ltd, Hong Kong
Printed and bound by Toppan Leefung Printing Ltd, China

This book can be ordered direct from the publisher at www.pavilionbooks.com

CONTENTS

INTRODUCTION

The term 'flower garden' might seem puzzling at first. Surely, by their very nature, all gardens are to some extent floral, whether they display just a handful of seasonal blooms or a riotous exhibition of colour. So what earns a garden the description of flower garden in particular? In researching this book I've had the opportunity to look closely at what it is that people enjoy most about growing flowers and the characteristics that unite the gardens they create. Whether they grow them as a cut flower or herb, or strictly for the ground or garden pot, nurturing flowers is for many people an act of immeasurable satisfaction.

Keeping any given area in bloom is no simple task; nearly all plants spend a great deal of their life neither in flower nor bud, the flowers being merely the climactic peak of their lifecycle. Where other gardens might give room to long-lasting evergreen forms, the flower garden devotes centre stage to a sequence of striking performers, creating maximum impact with a range of plants designed to bloom in sequence. This undertaking becomes even more impressive when you consider the gardeners who have applied the same principle to restricted spaces.

Over the course of six chapters, *My Tiny Flower Garden* explores the remarkable ways in which people have sought to accommodate flowers, often in unexpected circumstances. Whether by maximizing a display with inventive techniques or taking a resourceful approach to repurposing found objects, the gardeners in this book illustrate that no space is too small when it comes to making room for flowers. From jam-packed little borders to rooftop wild flowers, the 25 gardens featured here celebrate the diversity of flowering species and the many different ways in which we can benefit from them.

With practical tips and instructions, this book aims to demonstrate that flowers needn't require a large plot and that there are a great many ways in which to bring their captivating charms right to your doorstep. Ten projects show you how to make your own crafty plant containers, miniature meadows and even tea bags using your back-garden bounty. Celebrating the creativity and skill behind a host of floral triumphs, *My Tiny Flower Garden* hopes to inspire you to get stuck into your own patch, however large or small.

THE BLOCK
IN BLOOM

The act of gardening can be a great way to bring people together. Those without a growing space of their own often look to the community around them, and in so doing create some of the most innovative results. From an Italian floral street competition to community interventions bringing new life to city streets, the features in this chapter show how the tiniest of spaces can provide the loudest of statements. Is your neighbourhood lacking in horticultural spark? You may be the one who is ready to take action.

The streets of Spello are crammed full of flowers during the months of May and June.

SWEET STREET

Every year, thousands of people gather in the streets of an ancient village in central Italy to witness a spectacular event. Traditionally held on the ninth Sunday after Easter, the floral extravaganza in the little Umbrian hillside town of Spello enraptures visitors. This time-honoured custom, known as the Infiorate, takes place during the Catholic festival of Corpus Christi.

Working through the night on the eve of the celebration, hundreds of local participants group together to coat the roads in a floral carpet. With a mass of brightly coloured petals collected over the preceding months, each team paints a picture with flowers, depicting religious, historical and often philosophical themes. In the spirit of friendly competition, the Infiorate pictures are reviewed by a panel of judges and a winning team is chosen. There is, however, an accompanying Spello competition which offers residents a second chance at victory. It is this that I've come to see in this authentic, charming town.

Arriving on a warm, breezy afternoon, I meet Claudio, a native of Spello and enthusiastic participant in the contest. As we ascend the narrow, cobbled streets, he tells me how it developed. 'During the spring period we always have a lot of tourists who come to see the Infiorate. The idea therefore was to dress the whole town with flowers, from every veranda to each tiny side street, to make it beautiful for visitors.'

Now in its sixteenth year, it's clear that the idea has taken off in a big way. As we navigate slowly through the lavishly decorated alleyways, every direction we turn reveals a new and astonishing display. From brackets and balconies hang liberally planted baskets; doorways are smothered in the bright white blooms of star jasmine (*Trachelospermum jasminoides*) and every ledge available supports a plant pot or three. 'In late June the gardens are judged,' says Claudio. 'The winning displays are announced on the noticeboard in the main square, and successful participants are given congratulatory plaques.'

This is the second year that Claudio and his wife, Emanuela, have entered into the high-spirited festivities. Opening up the private entrance to their old-town Spello home, the couple have adorned their otherwise concealed courtyard with an arrangement of eye-catching plant pots. 'Last year we won second place,' says Claudio, pointing proudly to the plaque hanging beside the apartment stairwell. Taking an unconventional approach to their floral contribution this time, Claudio and Emanuela made a central feature from an ageing garden relic. 'My father's friend in the nearby village of Sellano made a wheelbarrow. After many years of use he asked if we'd like it for our own garden,' Claudio says. 'When we bought this apartment in Spello we decided to make it a centrepiece; now it works well for the flower competition.'

The competition is a chance for the whole town to get creative with containers, making use of hanging baskets to add height to their displays.

Coping well with the Italian heat, the plants include many varieties of petunia (far left) and tall, multi-headed stems of vibrant amaryllis (left).

Claudio has entered into the annual festivities by planting up his rustic wheelbarrow (right and below left). Visitors are encouraged to wander through into the colourfully decorated courtyard outside his Spello apartment.

With its rustic wooden panels and weathered, homely demeanour, the hard-wearing wheelbarrow makes for an ideal garden planter when filled with a layer of compost. Underplanted with ivy, a mixture of white and red impatiens festoon the compact barrow, catching the light at the centre of the courtyard. Repeating these two colours throughout the stairwell, Claudio and Emanuela's planting is at the same time lavish and refined. Impatiens is a town favourite, its long-lasting flowers performing reliably throughout the season. Other Spello stalwarts include similarly tenacious blooms such as pelargonium, verbena, begonia and zinnia, while impressively tall stems of striking amaryllis are an occasional feature on the doorsteps of participating households.

Back out in the bright, sunlit street, Claudio and I pass below a balcony overflowing with vivid petunias. 'We love our town and we love to dress it with flowers,' he says, 'it's in our DNA.'

*Sunflowers lift their giant
heads above their patch
at the top of the park.*

SUNNY HEIGHTS

When you think of sunflowers *en masse*, you probably visualize the fields of southern France. As those who have encountered them will agree, a sea of enormous yellow flowers swaying softly in the breeze is a sight to marvel at. For the locals of Waterlow Park in North London, however, a little piece of French farmland has been brought to their doorstep.

As co-ordinator of the park's volunteer group, garden designer Patricia Walby has been gardening at Waterlow for just over five years. A strong believer in the importance of green spaces in cities, she holds that flowers play a crucial role in the well-being of the public. 'When you pass by a beautifully kept flower bed you immediately feel as if the world is put to rights,' she says. 'The sensory pleasure of flowers is very restorative.'

With this in mind, Patricia and the volunteers embarked on a specific project that could educate as well as serve visitors to the park. 'We had this idea of inviting local schools to participate in growing sunflowers from seed, planting them here and then watching them develop into full-sized flowers. Most schools don't have the space to do that.' Testing out the process first so as to better understand how it could be conducted with small children, the group planted 400 seeds into pots, lined them out behind the park office, and regularly monitored their progress. 'Sunflowers are particularly good because they're big, they're blingy and they're pretty reliable,' Patricia says. 'Within the 400, we sampled six different varieties and achieved a germination rate of about 97–98 per cent.' The team then proceeded to plant out the seedlings on a sunny May morning in a 3 x 4m (10 x 13ft) section of the park.

Meeting once a week to carry out horticultural tasks in the park, the gardening volunteers spend time weeding and watering the sunflower bed.

'Having tried it out, we're now more confident with things like knowing when to repot, how best to plant out and how to obtain the maximum impact of the plants in flower,' Patricia says. And when it comes to maximum impact, no one could doubt the success of the project: the effect is stunning. Ranging in height, hue and texture, the sunflower patch forms a vibrant beacon, one to which you can't help but be drawn closer.

As Patricia explains, this simple exercise is intended to confront an issue with much wider social implications: 'A lot of children don't understand about the cycle of plant growth. Many think that in the winter a tree is dead, which is one of the causes of damage to young trees in the street. By engaging schools at an early stage we have the opportunity to introduce children to real plant cycles; to see something that they've created growing through the whole cycle. The hope is that it might teach them how to love and look after a park, for if ever there's been a time when urban people really need their green spaces it's now.'

The team tried a number of cultivars. Orange-petalled 'Earthwalker' (far left) is particularly striking.

Sunflowers come in many different forms, varying from giant to knee-high, bright and dazzling, to deep crimson and orange. It's therefore worth choosing varieties that will best suit your space: while raising enormous monsters from a tiny seed can be exhilarating, big isn't necessarily beautiful! Patricia and her team went for a range of sizes and colours, including the popular cultivars 'Sunbright' and 'Earthwalker'.

Beyond their beauty, sunflowers are also an excellent provider for the natural world. Because each flower head is made up of thousands of tiny flowers, they're jam-packed with nectar, attracting butterflies and bees. The latter stages of the plant cycle can also be of great importance for wildlife; sunflower seeds provide a food source for birds right through to winter, and they attract a wider range of species than any other seed. Allowing your sunflowers to fade and set seed where they stand is therefore a fantastic way to support the local habitat.

LAFAYETTE GREENS

Where there is a neighbourhood problem, the potential of solving it knows no limit when the solution has the backing of the residents themselves. At the centre of downtown Detroit, a mixture of historical architecture and gleaming modern towers, the once empty lot of a demolished skyscraper is now a shining example of realized potential.

Formerly the location of the stately Lafayette Building, the parcel of land was acquired by a Detroit-based software company, Compuware Corporation, just a block away. Envisioning a productive green space that would allow employees a chance to get out of the office and work alongside the community, Compuware enlisted the services of community arts curator Megan Heeres. 'I was brought in to spearhead the scheme,' Megan says. 'I'd call it a community project at corporate speed, because making a garden project happen that quickly was pretty unheard of in Detroit at the time.' Injecting both financial backing and momentum, Compuware founder Peter Karmanos Jr saw the space as a garden integrated within the city, its goal to provide a place for employees and local residents to meet each other and grow fresh produce and flowers.

The urban garden offers residents
the opportunity to grow fresh
produce in the heart of Detroit city.

With planters ranging in size, Lafayette Greens provides a place to garden for a diverse demographic.

Six years on, the garden known to Detroit residents as 'Lafayette Greens' is now a splash of colour in the surrounding city landscape. Rows of compact planters house a bright array of flowers and vegetables, capturing the attention of passers-by. With weekly volunteering sessions, Lafayette Greens is exemplary in its commitment to nurturing education along with the well-being of Detroit's downtown community. However, conceiving such a space was no easy task. Bringing in local landscape architect Kenneth Weikal, Megan began working towards a site plan that would best serve the diverse demographic who would be using it. 'It was very much a team effort,' she explains. 'I hired Gwen Meyer as the garden manager in the winter of 2011. We needed someone who not only knew how to grow, but cared about the aesthetics of a space. Gwen also brought a sense of generosity and empathy, and the ability to engage local people in genuine ways. 'This kind of engagement, as Gwen affirms, was at the

heart of the conception of Lafayette Greens. 'It was so important to us to include residents and families in our decision-making,' she says. 'It was essential that we encouraged continued involvement.'

When putting together Lafayette's design, Megan and her team looked to maintain aspects of the garden's former structure. The original Lafayette Building had been constructed in a triangular shape to allow as much natural light into its offices as possible and the arrangement of Compuware's garden needed to fit within the existing three-edged perimeter. It was also decided that the space should incorporate the natural walkways that had developed during the site's brief fallow period. Megan explains, 'The diagonal paths that cut through the garden reference the walking paths that people were using when the space was just an empty lot.' With this in mind, containers lining the main path were

planted with heavily scented lavender. 'Even if someone can only spend the shortest amount of time just cutting through the space, they can at least have an aromatherapeutic experience,' she adds.

With its rows of planters, Lafayette Greens takes the form of a potager garden, in which flowers, vegetables and herbs are all grown together. The flowers attract pollinators and beneficial insects, such as ladybirds and beetles, which in turn help the produce to prosper. Maintained by a wide network of volunteers, the garden has become a popular attraction for many Detroit residents. The chance to grow plants in the centre of the city has created new and exciting opportunities for people, as Megan explains. 'The beauty of the space is that it has allowed those who might not normally interact on a daily basis to have real human conversations and to start to break down some of the barriers that have been built up.'

THE HOOPLA GARDEN

When Will met Mak it was very much a meeting of minds. Brought together by a mutual friend, the two shared a vision of bringing green back to the city. When she opposed a planning notice which sought to privately develop an area of public land in her south London neighbourhood, Mak enlisted the local community. 'Unless we did something about it,' she says, 'we were going to lose one of the few green spaces available to us.'

Preserving the space as a public domain required an intervention of the most active nature: conceiving and assembling an alternative development which would better serve its residents. Mak says, 'I just wanted something different, something designed. As a landscape architect, Will was able to offer the language, the expertise and the know-how. He saw the potential in the space.'

Enlisting a small army of willing garden volunteers, it wasn't long before Will and Mak had erected what was to become the first of their many community garden projects. Crammed full of flowers and vegetable planters, the site was a great success, attracting interest from all across the area. Adopting the name 'The Edible Bus Stop', the green-fingered pair began looking for their next kerbside creation. 'We were approached by West Norwood Feast, who run a community fair,' says Mak. 'They told us that they'd liked what we'd done with our first edible bus stop, and

could we come and do something in West Norwood.' After conducting a survey of the area and holding numerous community consultations, this particular site was chosen.

Will picks up the story here: 'It was known locally as "The Bollards". There were lines upon lines of bollards added over time. The council had put them here as a means to get over a parking problem, but ended up creating a landmark.' Tackling the process of redesigning the space, Will and Mak decided that rather than remove the bollards, they would have fun with them instead. 'We created these large circular planting beds,' says Will. 'They look as if they've been thrown around the bollards like giant rings, which is how this came to be dubbed the 'Hoopla Garden'.' Incorporating the bollards, Will says, is a way in which the project has retained its local heritage, while giving it a fresh look. Just how community-centred a project it is becomes swiftly apparent as a local resident warmly greets Mak and Will, before disappearing to fetch us some water. Will introduces us: 'This is Frank, who keeps an eye on the beds. Frank's been involved since the garden began. It's fantastic to have the input of those in the immediate community.'

The circular 'Hoopla' planters reference the garden's former site, making a feature of the roadside bollards.

*Will and Mak's original
wildflower planting
palette has made
room for community-
planted additions such
as kniphofia (far left).*

Will and Mak are hoping to create more spaces like the Hoopla Garden, bringing flowers and vegetables to the streets of London.

To realize their vision, Mak and Will received financial support through numerous charities and local authority match-funding schemes. It was the organization Grow Wild, however, which assisted with the plant sourcing. With a mission to transform local spaces with the introduction of native, pollinator-friendly flowers, Grow Wild were the perfect sponsor for this South London project. Using plants such as cornflower, ox-eye daisy and dead-nettle, their aim was to bring the countryside into the city, offering a connection with wildflowers for those otherwise unable to access them. 'Many city residents haven't encountered countryside hedgerows before,' Mak says. 'We're trying to create associations with nature that wouldn't otherwise necessarily exist.'

Another unexpected outcome of the Hoopla Garden has been the way in which the community has taken possession of it. 'The hoops are continually evolving,' says Will. 'What's been great is arriving at the garden and seeing that new plants have mysteriously arrived – people have begun treating the place as their own.' As the planting has been topped up, it has gradually formed an avenue along the pavement, transforming the route taken by commuters and residents. 'It's providing a buffer between them and the road,' Will says, 'and the psychological benefits of green space are amazing. Sometimes we don't even notice how it makes us feel, it just raises our positivity levels.'

HOW TO:
MAKE A SEED BOMB

Is your neighbourhood in need of a little floral TLC? Let the guerrilla gardener in you run riot with this simple home-made seed bomb recipe. Seed bombs are the perfect way to extend the reach of your undercover horticultural interventions without the need for wire-cutters and a balaclava. Tossed into an unused street corner or a bare patch you've been eyeing up on the commute to work, a little seed bomb can make a big impact.

To make your seed bombs you'll need a wildflower seed mix, multipurpose potting compost, a mixing bowl and wooden spoon, a jug of water and clay powder. The last can be purchased from art suppliers and beauty treatment retailers.

1. Roughly measure out five parts clay powder to one part seed and one part compost. The total quantity of material is optional, depending on how many bombs you'd like to make.

2. Pour the ingredients into a large bowl and mix together with a wooden spoon.

3. Adding a small amount of water at intervals, bind the mixture together using your hands. Be sure to incorporate the water slowly so as to avoid the texture becoming soupy.

4. Taking a small amount of the mix at a time, roll it into balls in the palm of your hand.

5. Leave your seed bombs in a cool area to dry off a little before taking them out to do battle with the concrete!

Check up on your bomb sites. With the pre-moistened clay and compost the seeds have all the necessary components to start growing, though a little extra attention once in a while could prove helpful for the young plants. Seedlings may benefit from watering during particularly dry periods: a discreet squeeze of a water bottle as you pass by will help them on their way.

While any introduction of flowers to an otherwise sterile environment is a good thing, some plants will thrive better than others. A wildflower mix, particularly one comprising flowers native to your area, is a good choice. Not only are they suited to difficult growing conditions, they're unlikely to be invasive or to cause damage to infrastructure, such as building foundations.

GROWING WILD

Neat and tidy gardens are often designed to induce a sense of calm and tranquillity. However, some gardeners seek to find room for as many plants as possible, allowing their creativity to run riot. Whether they go for inventive planting or simply permit nature to take over, they prove that even the smallest of plots can be wild at heart. This chapter features a selection of people who have found a way to bring a little wildness to their horticultural creations. If it's variety you're after, a particular colour palette or an unusual planting scheme, take inspiration from these unconventional gardens.

Overlooking the River Thames, Portia's meadow combines a rich tapestry of seasonal blooms with architectural grasses such as Melica ciliata.

AN URBAN MEADOW

In most cases, conceiving a garden for a tricky and constricted terrain can be a source of frustration for garden designers. However, when she was offered the opportunity to transform the raised platform of a demolished building site, Portia Baker's response was, 'Fantastic!'

As a landscape architect, Portia has worked with Richmond Council on numerous garden redevelopments. 'There are pros and cons to working with a local authority, but the great advantage is being part of a team that includes engineers, arboriculturalists, ecologists, contractors and park staff. You're able to think more strategically,' she says. It's through consulting with such a wide breadth of expertise that parameters are agreed and Portia is able to find the right plants for the right space – and this is no ordinary space.

'We call this an urban meadow,' says Portia, 'because it's a balance between the wild and the cultivated.' Now vibrant with energy and colour, this little oasis sits on the foundations of a former river-view house, raised 2m (6½ft) above the ground. With a soil depth of only 30cm (12in), the compacted rubble below rendered this space unsuitable for any trees or shrubs, so Portia saw an opportunity to implement a flower-heavy design instead. The planting design process consisted of narrowing an initially large plant list down to some 30 flowering species and three grass species, with the aim of providing as long a flowering season as possible, with maximum visual impact. Looking across the garden, it's easy to see that the plants are thriving and hard to even imagine what stood here before. After just two years in the ground, the planting appears to have claimed its small stake of land at quite a pace. As the evening sunlight slips downstream, the vivid, swaying heads of echinacea, fennel and rudbeckia *en masse* contrast wonderfully with their urban surroundings.

Over the years, Portia has developed a patchwork technique whereby plants are repeated across a framework of squares. This allows planting combinations to be 'textiled' across an area of more or less any size, giving the effect of a wild meadow while at the same time distributing plants evenly. 'Malva is beautiful,' she says. 'When you mix it with early native ox-eye daisies, *Salvia nemorosa* 'Caradonna' and hardy geraniums you end up with a really pretty early summer picture.' And this is just one of the many seasonal combinations Portia has implemented here. In spring the garden is filled with the nodding heads of daffodil, allium and nectaroscordum bulbs, while late-flowering perennials ensure that the area continues its display through to the end of autumn. 'The rudbeckias have done amazingly well. They are fantastic because they go on flowering for three months,' she says.

Allium *'Purple Sensation' (top left) and* Nectaroscordum siculum *(bottom left) make for showy, nectar-rich forms during late spring.*

The meadow can be enjoyed by pedestrians on Petersham Road.

Portia Baker seated by her sunlit meadow.

A pretty picture isn't the only outcome Portia has in mind when designing a space like this, though; the encouragement of wildlife is also a matter of great importance. Working closely with local ecologists on each project she undertakes, Portia is always keen to provide sources of habitat and food for as much of the resident wildlife as possible. 'When it comes to flowers, species diversity is the best thing for wildlife so it's good to try different things out,' she says. 'And people too seem to respond to this garden. I think it's beautiful, even if I do say so myself. There's something a little bit wild about it.'

The Cleavers' blue shed provides a
colourful backdrop for
their wild garden.

ON THE MOVE

A garden is often the result of many years of care and attention, so giving it up can be one of the hardest parts of moving house. When Michael and Gerry Cleaver swapped their London life for the more tranquil location of Llandysul in Wales, they were faced with just this problem. 'We had quite a big garden in London,' says Gerry. 'We loved it very much, and there were so many plants that we didn't want to lose.'

So Gerry drew upon the oldest horticultural practice in the book. 'When I knew we were going to move I went round collecting seeds,' she says. 'We packed our favourite flowers into an envelope.' With the seeds sown directly into newly prepared flower beds, it didn't take long for the Cleavers' floral entourage to settle into their home. Blending beautifully with the lush, hillside backdrop, foxgloves, rose campions and daisies fill the little plot, surrounding an attractive shed at the centre of the garden.

'We inherited this shed from the previous owner,' Gerry tells me as we walk along a narrow path leading us through a mass of wild flowers. 'It used to be an art studio.' The original colour of the shed was a dark, weathered brown, so Michael and Gerry decided to give it a makeover. 'We just wanted to lighten it a bit, to give it some character. We then added plants to soften the colour.' Erupting from hanging pots, great bunches of pinkish-white lobelia complement the shed's duck-egg blue, blending equally well with tall, arching foxgloves that reach up from the beds below. 'The garden is north-facing,' adds Michael. 'So it contends with an enormous amount of shade.' Mirroring the flower-packed hedgerows of their surrounding country lanes, the Cleavers' garden is a wonderful reminder that shade needn't prohibit an abundance of cheerful colour. 'The plants are the stars,' says Michael, pointing out a large clump of bee-smothered comfrey (*Symphytum officinale*).

When tackling the renovation of their little plot, Gerry and Michael had a strong notion of the garden they wished to create. 'It needed to be a pleasant, attractive place to sit in,' says Gerry, 'somewhere to enjoy a glass of wine at the end of the day. We also wanted to be able to look out from the house and see flowers.' As the house was flanked entirely by well-rooted lawn, the Cleavers had quite a bit of ground work to do before they could get growing. After lifting the grass and fertilizing the soil with local cow manure, Michael proceeded to lay a simple path with stepping stones. Next to be added were the shrubs, providing the developing garden with a framework and a sense of structure over the winter months. Once these primary elements were in place, the Cleavers were ready to let loose their packets of ripe and ready seeds.

'One of the things I've noticed in Wales is that everything grows really strongly and quickly,' Gerry says. 'You would think that this garden has been here a lot longer than is the case.' This success may in part be down to the soil, as Michael explains. 'The soil we've got here is an acid clay. It's very rich and has a lovely dark brown colour. Acid clay soils are the most nutritious soil there is. You can grow pretty much anything on them.' This is a fact proudly exemplified by a multi-stemmed clump of meconopsis poppy. 'We tried them in London but they just didn't like it,' says Michael. 'They love it down here, though. I think it's also to do with the moisture; as Himalayan natives they enjoy a cool, damp climate, which makes this part of Wales ideal for them.'

The beauty of this garden lies in its relationship with the surrounding environment. 'I like to avoid red in the garden,' says Gerry. 'I much prefer the softer tones of pink, lilac, white and purple.' With plants such as pink campion, geranium and ox-eye daisy, the garden reflects the area's native flora. Gerry says, 'The daisies really thrive here. I wanted something that would tumble down the side of the wall, and they do just that.' To embellish their naturalistic planting, the Cleavers carefully selected plants such as heuchera, astrantia and phlox but they are already enjoying the sight of the garden developing along its own path. 'The thing I've noticed with creating gardens is that they're always much better than you plan. You think you have an idea and you try things out, but then nature takes over and looks after it for you,' says Gerry.

With the soft pinks of wild foxgloves (top left and bottom right) rising above a mass of white daisies, the Cleavers maintain a palette of mainly pastel colours in the garden.

FLOWER SHOW

A self-professed 'amateur' gardener, Janet Boulton found that her horticultural interests developed primarily through her career as an artist. Advised to visit the compact yet influential garden of the late Oxford plantswoman Anne Dexter, Janet began painting the first in a series of carefully chosen gardens. 'I'm naturally attracted to formality,' she explains. 'I went looking for it in the gardens; there's an underlying geometry in my work.'

Spending long summer holidays outdoors with an easel, Janet broadened the ambition of her artistic visits, embarking on short-stay residencies at the Villa la Pietra, a renaissance villa outside Florence, and at Barnsley House in Gloucestershire, where the late Rosemary Verey created her celebrated garden. 'I was learning all the time about gardening,' she says. 'I spent almost as much time going around with my camera as I did painting. The fundamental thing I learned from Rosemary Verey was that it was possible to bring an element of grandeur to a small space.'

The little oasis tucked behind Janet's house in Abingdon, Oxfordshire, is very much an artist's garden. Much like any work of art, a garden reflects both its creator's personality and the inspiration that has influenced its development. Evolving over time, Janet's garden exudes personality from every corner. 'I would never have made a garden like this if I had taken a design course,' Janet tells me, as we pass beneath a formidable arch of ivy. 'No trained designer would ever have put in an enormous willow tree!' Framing the entrance to her tranquil back-garden studio, the willow is counted among Janet's happy mistakes. 'The garden would be poorer without it,' she says. 'The mistakes all contribute to it not being formulaic.'

It was a working trip to one particular garden that inspired another unconventional element in Janet's own plot. Created by Ian and Sue Hamilton Finlay, the great Scottish garden of Little Sparta used poetry and humour in a way that appealed greatly to Janet's own artistic propensity. 'Again I came to the garden through art,' she explains. 'Ian was interested in Cubism, and had used it very cleverly at Little Sparta.' Over the course of 16 years spent painting the iconic garden, Janet's absorption of Finlay's sculpture led to the creation of many installations at home: 'I'm very interested in poetry and literature, so I was inspired to introduce some inscriptions into my own garden,' she says. Made from a variety of materials, especially glass, Janet's works interact with the planting and fill her garden with curiosities.

'Because I made this garden only for me, I've had complete freedom in how I did it,' says Janet. 'There are a number of pieces in the garden which are inspired by nostalgia.' Raised on a working farm during war-time England, Janet remembers traditional hay ricks, local village fêtes and being allowed to run wild in the fields. 'I had a very fortunate childhood. It was idyllic, in a way,' she says. Among the many works in the garden, perhaps the most evocative of the past is a piece named 'Flower Show'. Displaying a lavish collection of brightly coloured pot plants, Flower Show is a homage to one of the annual traditions of her childhood. 'I remember the village fête so well,' Janet says. 'I remember the high excitement about what happened in that marquee, the sheer variety of flowers that were exhibited.'

Having simplified much of the structural planting in her garden, Janet has made Flower Show a space in which she is able to exhibit her impulse floral purchases. 'Since I love picking up plants, I can put any daft thing I buy there. Flower Show is a memory of the free-for-all nature of those village flower shows, so it's my opportunity to indulge in a little flamboyance,' she says. With its assembly of planted terracotta pots, the miniature monument is a floral extravaganza. Large white cosmos beam out from behind a single pink dahlia, while dazzling phygelius catch the sunlight in their bright tubular florets. There's an intended lightheartedness in the jubilant collection of plants, epitomized by its miscellany; impatiens bedding plants clash delightfully with the red and white *Salvia* 'Hot Lips'. At the heart of Janet's Flower Show sits an inscribed glass dedication. 'I did quite a lot of research to get that letter form right,' says Janet. 'It's not classical like a lot of the lettering in the garden; there's a flowing prettiness about it. It's the sort of lettering you might use on a card to your mother.' Janet's creation is both evidence of a cheerful playfulness with plants and a reminder of the elemental wonder of our earliest encounter with flowers in our childhood days.

The vibrant blooms of Flower Show hark back to the village fêtes of Janet's childhood. Bright red Salvia 'Hot Lips' (far left) stands out alongside the pinks of cosmos and phygelius (top right).

Claire's little front garden is festooned with bluebells during the spring months.

SEE HOW THEY GROW

For some gardeners, the enjoyment of plants comes as much from watching their development as it does from the mature blooms. With more species on sale than ever before, and a wealth of information on how to create the 'instant garden', the more subtle characteristics of familiar plants can often be overlooked.

For Hampstead resident Claire Potter, gardening is an opportunity to observe; to watch the slow formation of flowers as they settle within their surroundings. 'It allows my mind to wander,' Claire says. 'While I'm with the plants, I am always moved by their beauty and how and where they choose to grow – in directions towards or away from the sun, into crevices and across walls.'

The wilful nature of plants is never better demonstrated than when wild flowers are allowed to proliferate, and Claire's garden is a fine example. Come springtime each year, the charming front garden of her home is given over to a sea of wild blues. 'There were already lots of bluebells in the back garden so one spring I decided to move the soil into the front and by the following year they were already coming up,' she says. As in many wildlife-friendly gardens on the fringes of large urban areas, Claire's bluebells are the Spanish variety first introduced to Britain by the Victorians. Although its hybridization with the common woodland bluebell (*Hyacinthoides non-scripta*) has led to some bad press, the Spanish bluebell (*H. hispanica*) is a spectacular sight within small city gardens.

Claire enjoys the element of seasonality in her garden. Spring is marked by the return of the bluebells each year.

'I love gardening,' says Claire. 'It reminds me of my childhood.' Introduced to the world of horticulture by her father, she developed a passion for plants from an early age. 'He was an exceptional gardener. I have wonderful memories of being outside with him and of my childhood gardens.' For Claire, flowers are a link to the natural world; a connection on her doorstep with the wider environment. 'I really enjoy the time-line of the garden. The bluebells just do their own thing; they mark the seasons for me in a way.'

Set upon the slope of one of Hampstead's one-time village roads, the 6sq. m (64½sq. ft) plot is typical of the raised townhouse gardens in the area. However, Claire made a conscious decision not to formalize its composition. 'I wanted to create a fairly unstructured garden in the front, using what was already there and adding plants and colours that I liked. My aim was for the garden to look as if it takes care of itself, because it mostly does.' With the bluebells flowering so prolifically during spring, one might imagine the space would look bare once they have finished. Not so; the next layer of planting is ready and waiting in the wings. 'They're followed by peonies,' Claire says, 'which look wonderful in early summer.'

Mature camellia shrubs join the striking, early-flowering bluebells, adding red and pink into the display. Like bluebells, camellias are shade-tolerant and therefore well suited for Claire's front garden.

Reproducing by both bulb and seed, bluebells are able to multiply quickly, resulting in a blanket effect. Given time, other species of bulb will achieve the same spreading result, including the wild daffodil (*Narcissus pseudonarcissus*) and grape hyacinth (*Muscari latifolium*). Bulb-based flowers of this nature are best cultivated in a moist yet well-drained soil, with an integrated layer of organic matter.

A mass of flowers in bloom at the same time creates an eye-catching display, making it hard to walk past without stopping to take it in. I ask Claire about the attention that her garden attracts in the neighbourhood. 'It is so lovely to speak to people passing by or receive a message from a neighbour who enjoys the garden,' she tells me. 'Talking about plants is a wonderful way to connect with people. It makes me happy as I too love to stop and look at gardens.'

A DAHLIA DISCOVERY

'I like to think I'm on the football pitch at Old Trafford, looking up into the stands,' says Geoff Hoyle, standing on his small patch of symbolic turf, surrounded by a sea of bright dahlias. 'People are always gobsmacked when they see this for the first time – they've never come across anything like it.'

It's easy to understand their surprise, for Geoff's small yet flower-crammed back garden in Stockport is something of a rarity. Save for an impressive lilac tree and a handful of bedding annuals, the planting is exclusively composed of dahlias – around 350 of them.

Once keen vegetable gardeners, Geoff and his wife Heather slowly began introducing flowers to their yearly seed list, making the most of the rich, fertile soil that had developed through years of organic vegetable growing. 'When my dad was getting toward the end of his life he decided he couldn't cope with his dahlias any more and gave me his tubers,' says Geoff. 'I planted them out and it quickly became obvious to me that you get far more bang for your buck from dahlias than from any other flower.' With a flowering period often spanning right through the summer and long into autumn, dahlias are a reliable source of colour in the border.

It was their vibrant colours that caused dahlias to fall victim to fashion trends. During their heyday in the early 1970s, the wide and sometimes garish span of dahlia varieties often featured in horticultural magazines and nursery catalogues. The thirst for new and exciting forms encompassing all shapes and sizes resulted in an array of flowers that often looked almost artificial, much like the colourful, showy bedding plants in favour at the time. Inevitably, as a more naturalistic style of planting crept back into fashion, dahlias gave ground to less ostentatious flowers.

Geoff deadheads all his dahlias. By removing spent flowers before they have time to drop petals, he makes room for fresh new blooms.

Geoff and Heather's back garden is a celebration of colour and form, displaying the huge range of dahlias.

Geoff has no patience with the fickle nature of horticultural trends, however. 'I can't imagine why anything like that would go out of fashion, or why people don't like vulgar colours,' he says. 'Perhaps that's how I am – a bit vulgar myself! But that's what appeals to me.'

Geoff enjoys growing bright, showy dahlias such as D. 'Chimacum Davi' (left) and D. 'Summer Festival' (below left), with its peach-centred petals.

Maintaining Geoff's collection of 150 varieties takes some doing. In colder climates such as the north of England, dahlias are at risk from the frost. Each year they require digging up, cleaning and packing away for the winter. Then there's the preparation they require prior to spring. Geoff uncovers the stored tubers and lays them out on trays in his greenhouse. As green shoots begin to show, he sets about segmenting, separating and propagating the rhizomatous roots, potting them up to grow on under cover, before finally planting them outdoors in May.

Having so many different and striking forms of dahlia lovingly cared for, carefully guided into flower and planted out in such density is what makes this little garden unique. Geoff tells me that most dahlia enthusiasts grow for exhibition, but this is a much less attractive proposition for him. 'They have them all growing in a poly tunnel, place one flower on show and that's it. I don't see the attraction myself. I say bang it in and get the colour!'

From the lavish, globular pompom dahlias to the more reserved, single-flowered, cosmos-like species such as *Dahlia merckii,* there are many dahlias to choose from. When you're working with limited space, however, deciding which to include becomes even more important. 'I've gradually built up a stock of plants that flower above the stem and are very strong and don't flop,' says Geoff. 'I've also found some that grow very tall, which has enabled me to create this wall of colour effect in the garden.'

Once the growing season is under way, a few key maintenance steps become crucial. Aside from requiring a healthy nutrient level in the soil, almost all non-dwarfed forms of dahlia will need staking. 'Deadheading is pretty important as well,' says Geoff. 'If the rain gets on the flower heads as they're going over, they look a mucky mess. I'm quite ruthless with the deadheading; I'll chop them off before they begin to turn.' And if snipping off flowers at their peak of exhibition feels somewhat barbaric, those of a reluctant hand can take courage in the fact that deadheading will repay with a wealth of fresh new buds.

You might think that so many plants squeezed into one space must put a strain on the watering can, but surprisingly Geoff says that his dahlias survive quite happily without the need for too much additional watering. 'Though,' he adds, 'as we're in Manchester we're not short of rain!'

At the peak of summer, the collection requires daily attention. Loose stems need to be tied in, and deadheading lavish blooms such as D. 'Pianella' (below), becomes an essential activity.

53

HOW TO: BRING YOUR DAHLIAS SAFELY THROUGH THE WINTER

Dahlias make a fantastic addition to even the smallest of gardens. With a vast range of sizes, forms and colours, these fast-growing, long-lasting triumphs have a great deal to offer. There are simple, single varieties such as the deep red *Dahlia* 'Bishop of Llandaff' and *D. merckii,* which displays modest pink flower heads on long, slender stems. Contrastingly, there are louder, flamboyant dahlias such *D.* 'Babylon Bronze', which catches the eye with its bright orange petals. Whichever category takes your fancy, a little extra care will keep them flowering year after year.

Originating from Mexico, dahlias are unaccustomed to the less sunny side of life. Therefore, if you're growing them in an environment prone to low temperatures, heavy frost or long damp winters, they stand a good chance of perishing if left to their own devices. There is, however, a simple technique that ensures they are kept healthy and happy throughout the worst of the winter weather.

1. Towards the end of autumn, as temperatures fall, you'll notice the growth of your dahlias slowing down. At this point, or just after the first frosts, lift the tubers from the ground using a garden fork and take them indoors. Carefully tap off the dirt and trim back the stems.

2. Placing the tubers upside-down, leave them in a cool room to dry for 4–5 days. Allow air to circulate around the tubers by putting them on a rack, such as an old kitchen strainer.

3. Line a plastic or wooden crate with fabric. This will be used to store your dahlias.

4. Place the dahlia tubers inside the crate and cover with ordinary potting compost. Store the crate somewhere dark, cool and dry.

Check on your tubers throughout the winter. It is important that they are not too damp (look for rot) or dry (showing signs of withering). As temperatures rise and the growth cycle begins to start up again, watch for signs of shoot development. This will indicate that the tubers will soon require potting up and bringing into the light. Be sure not to expose them to the outdoors until all signs of frost are over. Once the shoots have grown 30cm (12in) or so the dahlias will be ready for planting back into the ground.

ASKING
THE EXPERTS

Even the most experienced of horticulturists will agree that when it comes to gardening, there is always more to learn. A little shared knowledge goes a long way, especially when our growing space is limited and we want to make the most of it. Across the next few pages we shall meet experts in various horticultural fields who have applied big thinking to small spaces. Whether their own small sanctuaries were created from long-standing knowledge or by simple trial and error, the gardeners in this chapter discuss the ideas and techniques behind them, demonstrating that garden principles often remain the same irrespective of the size.

Gravetye Manor's Little Garden is a riot of colour in early summer.

MANOR HOUSE MEDLEY

Gravetye Manor in Sussex offers the very archetype of a flower garden, for the densely packed borders and ever-changing array of flowers spilling on to the paths make it hard to imagine one that could be more colourful and alive.

Originally the home of gardener and journalist William Robinson (1838–1935), proponent of the natural style of gardening that was in accord with the Arts and Crafts movement that flourished in the late 19th century, the manor house now serves as a boutique hotel and restaurant. Walking me down through a series of ornamental terraces, head gardener Tom Coward tells me how he came to be at the helm of this treasure trove of a garden. 'I've known Gravetye since I was 18,' he says. 'I used to visit a lot when a friend of mine became a gardener here.' So when the position of head gardener arose in 2010, Tom eagerly took it up. 'The garden was quite derelict. It was an amazing opportunity to renovate what has always been a very special garden for me, so it's been a dream job.'

One of the garden's stalwarts is Rosa glauca. *Clusters of candy-red flowers stand out against its dark, coppery foliage.*

Arching stems of dierama (right) spill over on to the path, the soft pink flowers harmonizing beautifully with the architecture.

Head gardener Tom Coward with loyal garden companion Vera (left). Ammi majus and achillea both make bright additions to the courtyard (below).

Tom sows a range of summer annuals from seed each year. Among those in the Little Garden are Papaver commutatum *'Ladybird' (far left) and* Eschscholzia californica *(left).*

Drawing on his experience of working in some of Britain's most celebrated and prestigious gardens, Tom has brought a wealth of knowledge and an attention to detail to Gravetye's complex planting. 'Our style is very full; we use very intense plantings,' he explains, as we enter a small courtyard at the manor's entrance known as the Little Garden. As a prime location for guests to enjoy breakfast and coffee outdoors, the Little Garden is one of the focal areas of the manor garden and a key space in which to demonstrate the elaborate planting. 'The hardest thing about gardening is that there are so many beautiful plants and always a limited space, and that's even more exaggerated in a small garden,' says Tom. 'Getting the proportions right is important. The size of the plants needs to be balanced with the scale of the space so that you don't feel squashed among them. At the same time I think you shouldn't be afraid to use some large plants in a small space. If everything is miniature the effect can be quite twee.' Indeed, far from appearing to further diminish the size of the Little Garden, a philadelphus with a mass of elegant, flower-laden stems demonstrates that by bringing in the element of height you can create rooms even within a very small area.

Surrounded almost entirely by a stone wall, the Little Garden forms a unique space within the wider garden. This has offered Tom the opportunity to experiment with a particular planting palette. 'You can use the climate in a small space to your advantage and select things that you wouldn't otherwise grow,' he explains. The warmer, protected environment lends itself to tender plants such as *Salvia involucrata* 'Bethellii', with its lavish, exuberant pink petals. Summer annuals also perform notably well here; growing up through the perennial planting are the entrancing flower heads of Californian poppy (*Eschscholzia californica*) and bishop's weed (*Ammi majus*). The dainty single dahlia *D. merckii* also draws the eye as it stands out against its confined backdrop. 'We play with germination timing as well,' Tom tells me. 'If you germinate *Ammi* in October they'll often reach a much greater size than those germinated in the spring.' Another horticultural technique employed in the courtyard is a timely prune of some of the herbaceous plants at the end of May. Key floral contributors, such as *Salvia* and *Thalictrum*, are lightly trimmed back, keeping them compact and producing twice as many flowers.

Heavily scented philadelphus blooms fill the garden with fragrance (bottom left), while dianthus (left) remain an integral feature within the planting.

'Scent by an entrance is also very important,' Tom says, 'especially in a small garden where the fragrance is trapped.' With this in mind, plants such as *Euphorbia mellifera*, philadelphus and heavily scented roses feature prominently in the Little Garden. 'That's the most primeval sense, isn't it?' says Tom. 'You might not even notice that you're smelling a particular plant, but it's triggering a memory from when you were six. That's the magic of gardens.'

The little walkway between Stephen's greenhouses is crammed full of attractive leaf forms such as the giant Canna *'Black Knight'.*

LEAFY LONDON

'I guess you'd call this a gardener's pleasure garden,' announces Stephen Crisp, standing in the utility walkway between a potting shed and three huge greenhouses. Dubbed the 'Pub Garden' by Stephen and his colleagues, this area of a prestigious central London garden became a source of lighthearted jest.

'We used to fill it with bedding plants and garden leftovers,' says Stephen. 'So the joke was that it was a bit like a pub garden. The vintage sign came from eBay – when I saw it I had to have it.' Fitted to the potting shed wall, the sign reads 'The Spade and Shovel', complementing the 'courtyard' perfectly. However, as time went by, Stephen began to play around with the awkward corridor, introducing a new, exotic dimension.

Evolving into a unique horticultural environment within the wider garden, Stephen's pub theme has given way to a more sophisticated concept. 'For me it's now all about leaf forms,' Stephen tells me. 'The emphasis in this space is on striking, exotic-looking foliage; plants that are not suitable elsewhere in the garden.' With its rich, dark coloration, an enormous *Canna* 'Black Knight' makes an instant impression. Celebrated for its distinctive red flowers, the plant is valued for its late summer peak. 'When it comes to flowering plants, their foliage is frequently overlooked,' explains Stephen. 'In fact, many of our floral favourites offer so much more by way of foliage.' Among such examples as *Persicaria*, *Geranium* and *Melianthus*, the 'Bishop' series of dahlias are one of Stephen's triumphs. 'Even when they are not in flower you've got this wonderful chocolate foliage. Very few things flower for more than two or three months, so if something has great foliage too you're probably going to have at least six months of interest.'

flowers in a vase except that you're working with plants in pots. When you have a space like this it's easy to move things around and make it look fresh again. It's like a stage set, really. That's the way I think of it; a bit of theatre.'

Stephen describes the theme of his corridor creation as exotic. However, this word carries associations that he thinks are often misleading. 'People don't realize that so many exotic-looking plants are actually very hardy and perform perfectly well in the garden in the UK,' he says. Cannas are a great example, but among others Stephen notes *Nerium oleander*. This Mediterranean shrub with attractive, blue-green lanceolate leaves, is often mistakenly assumed to be too tender for less warm climates. 'Oleander is much more robust than people think,' says Stephen. 'I've seen it flowering its heart out on a north-facing bank in a municipal car park!' Crucially, oleander delivers just as much splendour with its leaf form as it does with its showy flowers. 'For me,' concludes Stephen, 'good plant material is not good because it's rare or exotic, it's because it's high performance. And high performance is the key to making an attractive small space.'

The corridor has become a resting place for pots and plants alike that are unsuited for use in the garden. 'I tend to see things I like in nurseries and because I have this area, I can stick them in a pot. I then have an opportunity to try them out, and see how well they perform.' With a strong interest in floral design, Stephen enjoys nothing more than playing around with plant combinations, and the mobile nature of potted specimens lends itself well to creative experimentation. 'It's almost like arranging

Attached to the wall of the potting shed, the vintage pub sign (far left) is an indicator of the lightheartedness of the space.

CHALK MOUND

There can't be many scenes more profoundly attractive than a flower-rich meadow in summertime, for the sight of wild flowers intermingled *en masse* is innately captivating. Harking back to the traditional hay fields of pre-industrial England, Pam Lewis's meadows at Sticky Wicket in Dorset are a vignette of a forgotten landscape.

Sticky Wicket is a garden unlike any other. Dedicating it as a resource for British wildlife increasingly under threat, Pam has created a horticultural haven that places nature at its heart. Native perennial wildflowers typically flourish on poorer ground, where fertility-loving grasses present less of a problem by way of competition for space. With its nutrient-rich, heavy clay soil, Sticky Wicket is aptly named and Pam has had to apply expert knowledge and a great deal of patience to gradually deplete the fertility of her grassland pasture and return it to a vision of its flower-laden past.

However, there is a little section at Sticky Wicket that had a head start. Leading me through a farm gate and across a mown track, Pam reveals a meadow unlike the others. Tucked into a corner, a flower-festooned, 1.8m (6ft) mound of chalk stands out against the hedgerow. 'Chalk is the substrate that so many plants favour,' she tells me. 'Some of the best nectar plants will grow in chalky conditions.' Obtained from a nearby disused quarry, the chalk came with a supply of its own dormant seeds. 'That's what makes this special,' Pam says. 'It brought along elements of its own provenance which are local to this area.'

In creating the chalk mound, Pam (pictured far right) has provided a growing medium well suited to meadow favourites such as wild carrot, musk mallow and small scabious.

While all of Pam's meadows are a spectacle of floral diversity, the chalk mound is an exemplary feature. Awash with characterful flowers, the mound is a beacon for wildlife, providing a nectar-rich tapestry visited by butterflies, bees and beetles. Pam recites its resident flora and the list is stunning. Tall, swaying stems of hypericum, agrimony and wild carrot rise above a sea of colours; pinks and purples of knapweed, musk mallow and wild marjoram interweave among the yellow bedstraws and bird's-foot trefoil. Scabious and cranesbill bring soft blue to the mix, perforated by the bright white umbels of water dropwort. 'These are all plants that survive much better on a chalk meadow,' says Pam. 'The conditions are well suited to them.'

Having occupied Pam's field for over 15 years, the chalk mound is a source of continual change and development. 'This was the first chalk mound I made,' she tells me. 'I'd been wanting to try it out. We dumped the chalk in a heap and then slightly terraced it to encourage plants to establish.' Gradually settling over the course of a decade, the mound began to blend with its surrounding meadow. Although this has led to a more subtle, integrated appearance, the crossover makes its mark. 'There's a little more fertility on the lower regions, where the chalk has mixed with the clay,' Pam explains. 'The richest results in terms of flowers are on the top, where the substrate is purer. Lower down, the mound is grassier because it's picking up fertility from ground level.'

Another important factor when creating the mound was where to place it. 'It was always going to be good for bees,' says Pam, 'but butterflies often prefer a south-facing bank, so we needed to consider the aspect.' Once the mound was situated and the seeds sown, Pam allowed it to develop naturally.

Pam edits her meadows, removing false oat-grass, which often impedes flowers from proliferating.

'We have to keep an eye on false oat-grass,' says Pam. 'It can be a pain because it grows too high and flattens the other plants. You do have to edit a meadow, but it's hardly a gardening commitment!' Removing seed heads before they disperse, Pam keeps unwanted plants in check. This control method is simple and effective, although plants occasionally call for complete removal at the roots. 'We edit grasses more than any broad-leaved species in order to get the mix right,' she says.

Witnessing at first hand the results of Pam's labour, I find Sticky Wicket's meadows mesmerizing. However, achieved only via the application of traditional hay-meadow maintenance, this practice continually competes with the fertilizers of modern-day farming. Overcoming adversity, little creations like the chalk mound present an enormous benefit to wildlife. 'For anyone wanting to have a small wildflower patch in their garden without a struggle, chalk isn't the only option,' says Pam. 'You can use any limestone substrate or gravel or brick, as long as it's starved of nutrients.' Material of this nature, when crushed together, can provide the base for a meadow, however large or small. Once seed has been cast, it's then up to the plants to claim their ground. 'Species tend to knock each other out a bit and compete for space,' says Pam. 'You can provide a habitat for them but ultimately plants are wilful. They'll only go where they want to go, and they know what's best for them.'

1. Using short bamboo sticks and string, mark out the area you will be replacing with meadow.

HOW TO: SOW A WILDFLOWER MEADOW

Creating a meadow needn't require a field. In fact, there's no limit to how small a wildflower patch can be, so why not reinvent a sunny corner of the lawn with a little meadow of your own? There are many different types of meadow, the flower species depending upon the varying topography, so you will find many mixes available. In choosing a suitable site, consider the sunlight and rain exposure levels, as well as the drainage of the plot. You can then select your seed mix accordingly, making sure that you also obtain the right amount of seed to match the size of the plot.

Meadows are also a choice between perennial and annual. A perennial meadow will keep itself going year after year, provided it is managed and cut back accordingly. Conversely, an annual meadow is sown each year, and can often provide the brightest and most sensational display. Either way, the principles of sowing a meadow remain more or less the same, and with the right preparation the results are unbeatable.

5. Mix your chosen wildflower seed into a container of light, dry sand. The sand will help you to distribute the seed evenly, as well as indicating where seed has been sown once it is on the ground.

2. With a digging spade, cut along the string line to a depth of roughly 5–7.5cm (2–3in). The turf can then be shallow-cut and lifted.

3. Once the whole area has been removed, turn over the soil with a garden fork. This will loosen compacted ground and reveal any large stones in need of lifting and discarding.

4. Tread firmly over the soil to consolidate it before raking to a fine tilth.

6. Broadcast your seed and sand mix evenly across the exposed soil. It is advisable to water the ground prior to sowing to ensure that the seeds get off to a good start.

Once you've sown your mini-meadow, lightly tread the seed into the soil using flat-soled shoes. For a large-scale meadow this would be achieved using a roller, but for a smaller patch, feet of any size will do the job just as well!

Most meadow seed mixes comprise plants that are fairly drought-hardy, so once the seed has been sown, the area shouldn't require any further watering unless there has been a particularly dry period. In this case it would be advisable to give the ground a careful soak to make sure the seedlings do not dry out.

An annual flower mix will flower just once and then set seed before dying. This will mean cutting down the plants in autumn and resowing the meadow the following year. Ideally you should always allow the seed heads to form before you cut as they provide a food source for local wildlife. Poppies, which frequently feature in wildflower mixes, are a favourite among songbirds, such as dunnocks and sparrows.

SANCTUARY IN THE CITY

The public walkway that runs alongside Lambeth Road in the centre of London is one of the last places you might expect to find a produce garden. In fact, with a view across the Thames to Westminster Abbey and the Houses of Parliament, and overshadowed by the impressive towers and turrets of Lambeth Palace, this location couldn't feel any more metropolitan.

The garden of St Mary's is encircled by a brutal mass of tarmac and concrete, leading off the busy roundabout of Lambeth Bridge. Consequently, it takes the form of a much-needed sanctuary for local residents and tourists alike, providing a spot where they can briefly escape the mayhem of the bustling city. It is the dual project of both Lambeth Council and the Garden Museum, which was established to celebrate the history of gardening, its social importance and significant contributing figures. Given its close proximity and a desire to engage with the local community, the Garden Museum collaborated with the council to redesign this space, creating a garden that would rise above the expectations of a small municipal park. Wander through on a Saturday morning and you are likely to spot Aoife Power and her small army of volunteers hard at work. As the museum's gardener, Aoife dedicates a portion of her week to the upkeep of St Mary's Garden, with the assistance of a group of weekend helpers.

The flower cart greets visitors at the Garden Museum entrance, offering a chance to purchase a hand-picked and fresh bunch of cut flowers grown on site.

The cutting garden aspect is a recent addition. The museum had curated an exhibition exploring the history and significance of cut flowers in art, floristry and cultural tradition. With the thriving New Covent Garden Flower Market just down the road, the museum's gardening team began to think about the cut flower trade and some of the environmental issues that are implicated in growing flowers in sometimes unsuitable climates and importing them over long distances. 'We're so used to being able to purchase almost any variety of flower at any time that often we forget about elements such as seasonality, the way in which these flowers are grown and the road and air miles that go into supplying them,' says Aoife. The Garden Museum's response therefore was to grow their own, making use of the central ring of St Mary's Garden for creating rows of annual flowers and bulbs. 'The idea was to question what a cut flower should look like,' says Aoife. 'It needn't be a pristine rose from a supermarket, and actually it could be grown in your own back yard.'

The museum wanted the planting in St Mary's not only to be productive but also to encourage people to stop, sit and enjoy the garden. 'Although more contemporary produce gardens encourage mixed planting,' Aoife explains, 'we felt that lining plants in the traditional way with single rows exhibits a sense of order and control, which I think can be quite calming in a noisy and haphazard environment such as a city centre.'

Each week Aoife and the volunteers collect flowers into bunches and display them around the museum and on a specially designed flower cart at the entrance. For a small donation, visitors can choose a bunch to take home with them. The bouquets are varied, eye-catchingly colourful and about as 'local-fresh' as they come. 'The space dedicated for cut flowers is quite compact, so we had to think carefully about the kinds of flowers we would use. Our plant choices needed to ensure maximum output, repeat flowering and striking coloration, so our summer display includes plants such as dahlia, salvia, marigold, argyranthemum and tithonia,' says Aoife.

The compact produce garden is divided into three segments with box hedging. In the autumn spent rows are removed section by section and densely packed bulb displays replace the annual flowers.

POSIES
FOR SALE
PLEASE ENQUIRE INSIDE & PAY AT OUR FRONT DESK

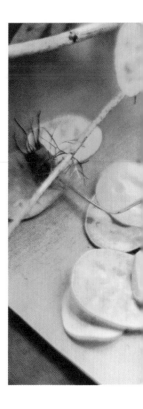

Aoife removes spent flowers from the growing beds and arranges new displays for sale on the flower cart (left).

Once the seed heads have been collected, the seed is separated and sown, bringing an element of sustainability to the project (above right).

Keeping cut flowers going year on year can end up proving costly on the seed front. Aoife combats this by allowing many of the annual plants to set seed at the end of the season, prior to their eventual move into the compost bin. By collecting and storing seed from flowers such as cosmos, tagetes and lunaria, a majority of plants in the cut flower garden can be supplied each year without having to buy in fresh seed. In addition, quite often the seeds and seed cases can look very beautiful in themselves, adding autumn and winter interest once much of the colour has faded in the beds.

'We reuse as many of our bulbs as possible each year, too,' says Aoife. 'Although tulips tend not to flower as reliably beyond their second season, we like to get the most out of them rather than throwing them away. As soon as a row has come to the end of its collective flowering period, the plants are dug up, heeled temporarily into a crate of soil and the foliage is allowed to die back naturally. This means the bulbs act as they would in the wild while at the same time being removed from the display area.'

The other thing to remember with a cut flower garden is that you are growing a crop, and much like any farmer's field or vegetable garden where annuals are grown, harvested and removed from the ground entirely, soil quality is the highest priority. Aoife ensures that each autumn, once the bulbs have been planted out, a good layer of organic compost is spread on top and dug in between the rows. 'A great proportion of the soil nutrient content is taken up by these plants every year, so it is important to replace it in equal measure.' Adding organic matter also helps to improve the soil structure itself, which is important when you're regularly disrupting it with digging and raking.

1. Bring your tender plant in from the garden. This example shows an *Argyranthemum* 'Jamaica Primrose' that has been grown in a pot.

HOW TO: TAKE SEMI-RIPE CUTTINGS

Some of the brightest and most prolific displays in the flower garden are achieved by the inclusion of tender plants. The vibrant colours of favourites such as dahlias, salvias and verbenas can transform the smallest of gardens, adding a seasonal boost to lift the spirits. As suggested by the name, however, tender plants are not best suited to battling the elements. When the days begin to shorten you will need to bring them in from the cold and take cuttings from them to provide replacements that will flower just as profusely the following year.

Even if you are growing these plants in a sheltered environment, such as a conservatory or greenhouse – or are fortunate enough to enjoy a warmer climate all year round – semi-ripe cuttings are still a fantastic way to replenish your stock.

5. Take a small pot with a depth of at least 7.5cm (3in) and fill with multipurpose compost. Pat the compost down and poke three holes using a dibber or the butt of a pencil.

2. Look for a healthy, non-flowering stem of roughly pencil thickness. Using a pair of sharp secateurs, make a cut below a leaf, giving you a cut stem about 7.5–10cm (3–4in) long.

3. Make a closer cut just below the base of a bottom leaf, then trim off the rest of the lower leaves. In order to prevent loss of water through evaporation later on, reduce the leaves at the top to just a few as well.

4. Dip the bottom of your cut stem in hormone rooting powder, which will aid initial root growth. Follow the same steps to produce two more cut and prepared stems.

6. Lower your three cuttings into the holes and very lightly firm them in place. Water the pot thoroughly and place in a warm and light environment, such as a heated greenhouse, conservatory or window sill.

Keep a close eye on your cuttings when it comes to watering. Over-watering can lead to a build-up of fungus which can be harmful to the soft plant material. Therefore, a good soak from time to time will suit them much better than continued saturation.

After a few weeks the cuttings should have already begun to develop new roots. Carefully check on their progress by tapping out the pot into your hand, being careful not to disrupt the new growth. Once the roots appear well established, divide your three plants and pot them on in separate containers.

Wait until all risk of cold weather is past before you transfer your new plants to the garden. In the meantime, pinch out developing flower buds so as to produce larger, branching stems prior to planting.

THINKING
OUTSIDE
THE BOX

For many of us, there simply isn't enough room to create the flower beds we would like. Growing in containers offers a simple way to satisfy our green-fingered fancies. But why stick to the conventional plant pots? As long as the basic requirements are provided, you'll find that plants are not fussy about the spaces they're grown in, and there's an opportunity to get crafty with some of the least likely items. With a range of alternative planters and tips for maximizing their floral capacity, the gardeners in this chapter present a new take on an old convention.

Mixing a bright array of flowers, Alex's reclaimed trunk is an eye-catching feature outside his shop.

TRUNK TREASURES

Alex Hales certainly knows a thing or two when it comes to floral displays; from assisting with award-winning exhibitions at the RHS Chelsea Flower Show to making his own bespoke arrangements for weddings and public events, he has created many an eye-catching design.

Well-known to residents of the Welsh coastal town of Aberystwyth, his boutique little flower shop, No. 21, is the workshop for Alex's imaginative schemes. 'I love coming up with new combinations,' he says. 'There's something addictive about working with flowers, something endlessly pleasing. With so many forms and colours to play with, there's always a great pairing just waiting to be discovered.'

Alex nursed a passion for plants from a young age and later studied horticulture at the National Botanic Garden of Wales; opening a florist was something he had always wanted to do. With its stylishly decorated interior and elegant selection of cut flower stems, Alex's shop is a botanical treasure trove, offering a wealth of ornamental inspiration. However, it is the recent addition at No. 21 that has been catching the attention of passers-by. 'The success of the flower trunk has been a total surprise,' Alex tells me. 'I had no idea it would attract so much interest!' When he stumbled upon the old trunk for sale, Alex set his plant-matching mind to creating a miniature flower bed within its four wooden walls. 'I'd been looking for a way to devise a planted scheme at the front of the shop. Cut flower displays are one thing, but I wanted something more permanent, something with vitality.' The vintage trunk offered Alex a chance to put his practical gardening experience to task.

Alex gets crafty with a smaller incarnation of his planted vintage container.

Very much in keeping with the vintage-chic character of the shop, Alex's planted trunk sits comfortably among No. 21's floral displays. Bringing together a planting scheme that could be applied to one's own sunny border, the trunk garden offers customers more than a simple bouquet. 'People seem to love it,' he says. 'I had never thought of displaying plants like this before. I think it demonstrates what can be achieved with a small space and encourages people to try new things in their flower beds.'

In order for Alex's trunk to be plant-ready a few alterations had to be made, especially to the base. 'We're in West Wales, so rainwater is not in short supply,' he says. 'With any compact planter, drainage is essential.' Having drilled 1.25cm (½in) holes in the wooden floor and the base of the plastic sheet lining the trunk to protect the wood from saturation and subsequent rotting, Alex filled the bottom section with lightweight clay pellets. Allowing water to drain freely, this kind of aggregate makes for an airy, lighter alternative to bulky material, such as grit or broken crockery. 'As the trunk would be standing out on the pavement, I wanted to avoid any unnecessary weight,' he explains. 'I knew I'd need to move it from time to time.' For the same reason, Alex avoided using too deep a layer of compost when it came to filling the trunk. He opted for a rich, moisture-retentive soil medium so that the plants would be able to establish without the need for excess earth. 'You can use any old plastic liner. Without one at all you'll vastly reduce the life of a wooden plant container,' he says.

Extending beyond cut flowers for the vase, No.21 is a treasure trove of horticultural inspiration.

Once Alex had prepared the planter, next came the fun stage. 'There's a nursery nearby with a great selection of perennials,' says Alex. 'I went looking for contrasting plant forms, as opposed to focusing on any particular colour scheme.' With this in mind, Alex's plant list includes the large, round heads of *Achillea millefolium* 'Summer Fruits Lemon', with their striking mass of yellow florets. Offsetting these tall, flat-headed blooms are the wilder forms of flower, such as cornflower and chicory. 'Chicory has always been a favourite of mine,' Alex says. 'It's often forgotten in residential garden planting. When you see it growing in the wild the blue is so captivating.' The trunk was therefore an opportunity for Alex to profile specific flowers, showcasing them alongside the more typical garden classics such as agapanthus and cosmos. 'It's like a Chelsea Flower Show garden in miniature,' says Alex, 'although I've managed to resist the urge to get at it with the manicure scissors!'

Having trained as a gardener, Alex enjoys any opportunity to experiment with planting combinations. Cosmos bipinnatus *is a particular annual favourite, ranging from white to magenta.*

1. Choose an unwanted utility case – a briefcase, vanity case or, as in this example, a well-worn typewriter satchel all make for suitable containers. You will also require a coir brick, cactus compost, horticultural grit, a jug of water and a range of flowering cacti and succulent plants.

5. Mix the coir and cactus compost together so that they are well integrated. Fill the middle third of the case with the compost mixture.

HOW TO: BRING A VINTAGE CASE BACK TO LIFE AS A SUCCULENT GARDEN

Here's a great way to transform an old utility case into a windowsill wonderland. Succulents and cacti are not immediately associated with floral exuberance, but these curious and often other-worldly plants pack some surprisingly beautiful and exotic flowers. Finding the perfect way to show them off can often be a challenge, so try giving an old appliance a makeover by following these simple steps to turn a vintage container into an indoor garden.

2. Fill the bottom third of the case with horticultural grit, putting half of the grit aside for later.

3. Place the coir brick in a bowl and pour water over it. As the brick soaks up water, it will begin to disintegrate. Loosen it further by hand.

4. Once the brick has been crumbled, add two generous handfuls of cactus compost.

Predominantly plants from desert and rock habitats, succulents and cacti dislike damp conditions so it's important that watering is done sparingly; check the saturation levels each time before topping up.

These plants also require plenty of sunlight in order to produce strong, healthy flowers, so be sure to position them in a bright spot by a sunny window.

6. Using your hands, press down on the compost mixture to firm the surface.

7. Arrange your succulents and cacti on the surface before proceeding to plant them. Ensure that each plant is well bedded in.

Planting bulbs in containers is a great way to brighten up a dull corner.

POTTERING AROUND

The wonderful thing about growing flowers in pots is that you can keep trying out new ideas. Like most gardeners, I have certain favourites – flowers I've been continuing with year upon year for their structure, colour and scent. But it's the act of experimenting in a garden that I find the most exciting, and getting a plant combination right can be enormously satisfying. Writing this book offered the perfect opportunity to share what I have discovered.

As a gardener, one of my favourite exercises in the flower garden has always been playing around with the herbaceous border. It's a process that requires planning, an understanding of individual plant characteristics and a level of patience, since plants need time to develop and spread in order to achieve their full potential in any given space. Growing in pots speeds up this process, and being able to dismantle a display and then reorganize it while the plants are in flower can be a lot of fun.

My London garden is only a few square metres of gravel. When I moved in I brought all of my pots with me, knowing I would want to grow whatever I could in the limited space available. Over the years I've amassed quite a few in all shapes and sizes, finding them at furniture markets or being given them by friends and family. There is usually a handful of empties stashed to one side so that I can add in new plants to replace those which have begun to die back.

95

Perennial daisies (Bellis perennis) complement the spring bulb display with dazzling flowers and deep green foliage.

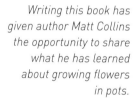

Writing this book has given author Matt Collins the opportunity to share what he has learned about growing flowers in pots.

Early on in my horticultural career I went to visit the Great Dixter garden in the south-east of England. It is renowned for its impressive and eclectic plant list and flower displays, and I remember being completely stunned by the pot arrangements on exhibition. Their use of contrasting colour and form exuded a sense of playfulness and enjoyment, demonstrating what can be achieved beyond simple bedding planting. Being creative in this way has remained one of the elements I enjoy most as a gardener, and there's no space too small in which to try out ideas.

Spring is a great season for potted plants. Bulbs in particular grow very well in containers and with so many to choose from, there's no limit to the combinations you can create. I really enjoy mixing bulbs together, coming up with simple pairings of particular varieties. Richly coloured tulips such as *Tulipa* 'Cairo' and *T.* 'Hemisphere' make striking backdrops for the softer, more delicate and scented daffodils such as *Narcissus* 'Cheerfulness' and *N.* 'Avalanche'. It's great also to mix bulb-heavy pots alongside those planted up with reliable biennials such as forget-me-not and purple scabious. Spring flowers often come in such bright and lively tones that it's quite easy to cultivate a varied array of interesting forms.

A problem with autumn-planted bulbs, particularly those in shallow containers, is that they are often at the mercy of autumn-foraging rodents, such as squirrels and mice. There are many prevention methods for tackling this, ranging from a top-scattering of prickly holly leaves to rolling the bulbs in chilli powder. I have even encountered a method that involved grating a paraffin-soaked firelighter onto the surface of the compost! For me, however, the best approach has been to simply cover each pot with a sheet of 13mm (½in) chicken wire and weigh it down with a heavy stone or brick. By the time the leaves have grown through it and reached about 30cm (12in) in height the danger period has usually passed, leaving the bulbs to grow on undisturbed.

1. Choose a good-sized pot and a selection of your preferred bulbs. You'll also need potting compost, drainage material, such as grit or broken crockery and a few bedding plants to top your display and give your pot a floral head start.

HOW TO: GET THE MOST OUT OF YOUR SPRING PLANT POTS

It's often difficult to choose between the many varieties of bulb on sale at garden centres and nurseries or in the autumn catalogues. But why limit your garden containers to just one display? By following this simple layering technique, you can ensure a bountiful colour array that will continue to impress throughout the spring months. Whether your favourites are modest daffodils, lavish tulips or delicate grape hyacinths, here's a great way to combine the lot!

Different types of bulb have different flowering times, so a careful selection will offer a sequential display that's easy to achieve. It's always best to check with the supplier if you're unsure of a particular bulb's flowering period. For my pot I've used nine *Narcissus* 'Pueblo', five *Tulipa* 'Montreux', four *T.* 'Ruby Prince' and 20–25 *Muscari azureum*.

5. Leaving the tulip tips exposed, add another layer of compost and place the muscari bulbs around them. You can be liberal with the quantity – they're only small!

2. Fill the bottom of your pot with about 2.5cm (1in) of crockery. It is important that water can drain freely to prevent the bulbs from rotting.

3. Add a thick layer of compost and place the narcissi on top. Space the bulbs far enough apart that they do not touch and check that the tips are pointing directly upwards.

4. Now add another layer of compost, making sure that the narcissi tips protrude just above the surface. Avoiding the narcissi tips, place a layer of tulips in amongst them. Here I have mixed together both tulip varieties.

Keep an eye on the weather. Once the sun is shining and the bulbs are in leaf, they'll need a little help to continue healthy growth. As there are many plants crammed into a small area it is important to give them enough water to avoid them drying out. Topping up the nutrient levels is also recommended; a single dose of liquid feed mixed into a watering can will be well received.

As the flowers begin to fade and drop their petals, deadhead them from the base of the stalk. This will keep the display looking its best while making room for the next layer of bulbs.

6. Add a final layer of compost and top-plant with bedding such as viola, forget-me-not and primrose, then water your pot.

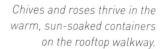

A BANK OF FLOWERS

The fire escape of a central London bank is the last place you'd expect to find a garden, let alone one producing a high-quality crop of edibles and flowers. However, the headquarters of private bank Coutts has seen its four narrow rooftop avenues adorned with planting containers of all sizes, crammed full of cooking ingredients for their in-house restaurant.

Walking me through his bustling kitchen and out onto the roof, Coutts' Head Chef Peter Fiori tells me where the story began. 'Until recently this was a dead space,' he says. 'I'd always wanted to do something with it, and Richard had the know-how.' He is referring to the expert micro-salad grower Richard Vine, to whom the bank's Skyline Garden owes much. Prior to his death in 2015, Richard spent two years developing Peter's dream of a kitchen-garden roof, resolving issues concerning space, irrigation, drainage and plant productivity. 'We shared the vision,' Peter says. 'This particular avenue used to be known as the Meadow Garden, but we've renamed it Vine Lane so that Richard's legacy lives on.'

As he grew up in a family of Italian farmers, a working kitchen garden close to hand is something Peter is very well acquainted with. 'Plants lose around 90 per cent of nutrients after 24 hours,' Peter tells me, 'so for optimum culinary flavour, the aim is to harvest roughly two hours prior to service.' This is something his kitchen team are now able to achieve, and the range of ingredients available to them really is impressive.

Head chef Peter Fiori stands among pots of French lavender, overlooking central London.

From herbs and salad leaves to plums and potatoes, the roof garden makes an enormous contribution to the kitchen's requirements. Recent additions have even included peaches and wasabi. 'We have everything we need without the air miles,' Peter says. And he has taken the kitchen garden a step further; making use of every facet of the roof's architecture, he and his team have managed to accommodate a staggering wealth of flowers, each one with either a culinary or decorative use. 'Camomile and lavender!' Peter exclaims, as we process along the walkway in single file. 'Now that's a combination. We blend them together as a syrup which goes perfectly with duck.'

The Skyline Garden is a great ambassador for the versatility of culinary flowers. Of course there are the usual species found in a kitchen garden; nasturtium and chive flowers, for example. However, Peter has found room for some of the less typical edible blooms that his intricate dishes depend upon. 'Fresh watercress flowers are amazing to cook with,' he says. 'The moment they hit a warm plate their aroma fills the room.'

Facing out from each aspect of the building, the garden lanes are exposed to differing levels of sunlight. 'The sun determines what we plant,' Peter says. 'We've recorded temperatures of up to 45°C (113°F) in one particular spot; with heat coming off the walls as well as from the ventilation ducts, it's like a little microclimate. During the first two years we were doing all the watering by hand. The soil is organic and peat-free, which means it can dry out quite quickly. Thankfully we've now installed an irrigation system, which can supply water across the roof to all of the containers.'

With so many plants blooming during the peak growing season, cropping requires attention to detail. 'All the chefs here are trained in harvesting our produce,' Peter says. 'They're taught when and how to cut, how to preserve the plant and maintain its shape too. Just five years ago I myself wouldn't even have known what half of these flowers were!'

Peter's staff have been trained in how best to harvest flowers from the kitchen planters. Nasturtium (left) is a particularly versatile culinary component.

CRAFTY CONTAINERS

Mauro Rettori's modest rustic wine shop sits at the heart of one of Italy's most celebrated wine regions. Deep-rooted residents of the sunny hillside town of Montefalco, Mauro's family sell premier wine produced exclusively in the area, operating from their boutique outlet at the foot of the old town.

Although its interior may conform to the typical appearance of a traditional wine seller's shop, the front of Mauro's is anything but conventional. 'The idea behind the crates came to me late one night while I was lying in bed,' he says. 'I'd been looking for a way to bring the shop to life and make it more colourful on the outside.'

With stock moving regularly through the shop, a wide range of transportation and packaging materials had begun to accumulate. Getting handy with a hammer and drill, Mauro saw a way to recycle some of these shabby wooden receptacles and create hard-wearing growing containers for a floral display. 'Flowers are important to me, they've always made me smile,' he tells me, standing amid a bright assembly of blooms. On his right is an old chestnut stock pallet, its mid-sections filled with compost, creating miniature flower beds that erupt with colour. Repurposing wine crates of differing sizes, Mauro has made room to house a profusion of showy plants. From the spires of heavily scented lavender to the blowsy, flamboyant petals of petunias and coreopsis, the eye-catching display spills out into the street.

An abundance of petunias cascade over
Mauro Rettori's container-clad bicycle.

Expanding on the theme, Mauro found yet another challenge for his up-cycling skills. 'The bike is my invention, it's a little more personal,' he says. 'I worked on it in my garage, fitting it with crates and hanging baskets. I wanted to create something loud and fun that would generate maximum impact. I've named the bike Calendula.'

Among the more intricate incarnations within the shop's repurposed display are a set of individual wine boxes, fixed to the entrance wall. Having cut the lids in half with a hinge on each side, Mauro has filled the lower sections with compost, creating little windowed containers for single plants. This is a great way to produce ornamental flower boxes, bringing a bare wall to life with tiny splashes of vivid colour. By drilling a handful of little holes in the bottom of the boxes, water can drain freely, ensuring that the plants do not sit in damp conditions. The screw fixings themselves were easily drilled when the lid was wide open but are now hidden from view.

'All the wine we sell is grown in the area,' says Mauro, 'so I wanted to use flowers from the area too. The majority of the display came from just outside Montefalco and a local plant seller supplied the lavender.' By using plants well suited to the warm, humid climate, Mauro's arrangements are quick to put on growth and produce a great wealth of blooms. Petunias make up the bulk of the display, tumbling over the crates in a range of radiant colours. With their lightweight stems and soft, tender flowers, they are the ideal choice when it comes to small containers such as window boxes and wall pots.

When selecting the plants for his vintage flower boxes, choosing brilliant, dazzling colours was very much an integral part of the decision for Mauro. 'My life is very colourful,' he says. 'I love my job, and I'm proud of the work that I do. In a way the flowers complement my life; they're an extension of my happiness.'

With simple alterations, the crates in Mauro's display have all been equipped to accommodate a striking arrangement of bedding plants. Strips of wood are attached at the base of the pallet lengths, creating miniature shelves.

1. You'll need ordinary potting compost, horticultural or 'weed-suppressant' fabric, scissors, a brush, paint, a staple gun (or hammer and small metal tacks) and, of course, a wooden pallet – ideally, one free of any rusty nails or sharp wooden splinters.

5. You're now ready to fill the pallet with compost. It's best to do this with the pallet upright, leaning on a wall. This way you can fill it from the bottom up, packing the compost in tightly as you go.

HOW TO: CONVERT A PACKAGING PALLET INTO A FLORAL WALL

A great way to brighten up a wall or garden fence is to make creative use of a wooden pallet. With its horizontal slats acting as individual shelves, a converted pallet makes for a multi-storey planter that will cascade with flowers. Whether you choose to plug-plant with instant bedding or make an early start with seeds, a pallet garden can be a fantastic addition to any restricted outdoor space.

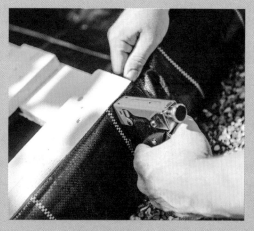

2. Paint the pallet a colour of your choice. Although it's not an absolute necessity, painting will help to lengthen the lifespan of the wood and to give the framework a general sprucing-up, too.

3. Fold your horticultural fabric to a size just wider than the pallet, so that the sides will wrap around the edges with ease.

4. Using a staple gun or small metal tacks, fasten the fabric to the back and sides of the pallet, leaving the front exposed. Cutting the fabric at the corners will help you to fold and fasten it neatly.

Keep an eye on the development of your pallet plants. Because the horticultural fabric will make it difficult for rainwater to soak down through the planted layers, it is important to water them regularly by hand. A good, careful soak once every few days will prevent roots from drying out.

Over time it is likely that the compost level will sink. Check to see that the plants are happily bedded in and top up the soil level if necessary.

6. Plant up your pallet garden with plug plants. You can do this with the pallet either standing or flat on the ground. I find that summer annuals, such as petunia, calibrachoa and lobelia cope well with the growing conditions.

7. Topping up your plug planting with a handful of nasturtium or calendula seeds sown directly into the pallet compost will bring even more variety to your floral display.

BEYOND THE GARDEN

Creating a flower garden can be enormously satisfying, but there are many ways in which to give your blooms a second life. Whether they are destined for the vase or preserved for a whole lifetime, flowers can extend their attraction far beyond their place in the soil. Each feature in this chapter presents a different approach to getting the most out of our horticultural endeavours, be it an exuberant cut flower display, a revitalizing herbal beverage or even an entire business. However small your garden may be, reap the benefits of your blooms by adding an extra dimension.

NEIGHBOURHOOD WATCH

The streets are glowing with the rich colours of autumn as I drive through the Parkdale neighbourhood of suburban Toronto. Leaves of deep yellow, orange and red litter the pathways and there's a chill in the October air. My arrival could not have been better timed for catching the famous Canadian fall, but despite the late season, the trees aren't the only plants bringing colour to these residential avenues.

Sarah Nixon, a self-professed 'flower farmer', has spent 12 years transforming some of Toronto's small suburban front gardens into places of floral abundance. Harvesting home-grown, organic flowers from her backyard, Sarah first began selling bouquets at produce markets. 'I became obsessed,' she tells me. 'I needed more room to grow in the city, and when you look around you see so much unused yard space.' So Sarah turned to nearby friends and neighbours. Given free rein to remodel and reshape a handful of gardens in which she could plant high-yielding flowers, she found her stock levels increased. The more flowers she was able to squeeze into a garden, the more spectacular it looked, and with a blooming portfolio of impressive front yards, it wasn't long before Sarah built up the confidence to approach strangers also. 'I say that I will plant tonnes of flowers and they won't have to pay for anything nor lift a finger, not even to water the plants. They'll get to enjoy the flowers without having to do anything.' And in return for her labour, Sarah visits each garden three mornings a week with secateurs and a bucket.

The idea of using urban gardens to grow flowers on a large scale came to Sarah first as a response to the burgeoning global market for cut flowers. 'When flowers have been flown in from places such as Ecuador and Holland, they've been packed dry for a week or so already, before they even reach the florist,' she explains. 'Whenever I buy flowers I notice such a difference in the energy. The flowers in my backyard are just so much more vibrant, diverse and irregular. Flowers that have been transported over long distances are usually very straight and all exactly the same, whereas my ones will have some curve and bend, which makes them so much more interesting to design with.'

This street is typical of the Parkdale district of Toronto in autumn. Long-lasting summer annuals flower through to October.

Together with Sarah I visited several of her flower gardens, all within a short distance of her house, and her floral workshop. Each garden offered different planting conditions, such as aspect, elevation, soil depth and access. In working with these varying factors Sarah is able to find the right growing environments for the right plants. While one garden may house a profusion of dahlias, another accommodates a lively combination of zinnias and foxgloves. Despite the differences, however, each of the front yards stands out proudly along the street, catching the sun in a kaleidoscope of colour.

Growing up on Vancouver Island, Sarah spent many of her summers working in an organic farm close to the family home. The resulting love of growing was what later drew her attention to an urban vegetable-growing scheme initiated by residents in the Saskatchewan city of Saskatoon. They were cultivating other people's front yards and offering a portion of vegetables as payment for using the space, and Sarah adopted this method, applying it to cut flowers. 'At the time no one else was really doing it,' she says, 'but there's a growing appreciation for local flowers now, after the local food movement has become so popular.'

High-yielding plants such as Cosmos bipinnatus *(left) and* Dahlia 'Lakeview Peach Fuzz' *(top left) provide a regular crop for Sarah.*

Sarah uses bamboo canes to stake dahlias. Producing a great wealth of orange pompom heads, this plant requires sturdy support.

Having developed her cut flower business under the name My Luscious Backyard, Sarah has expanded her retailing reach beyond local farmers' markets. Toronto residents can purchase Sarah's seasonal, low-mileage blooms in nearby florists and subscribe to weekly bouquet deliveries to the home or office. Sarah also offers flower arrangements for weddings and other events. 'My gardens really get going in June with the growing season lasting roughly 19 weeks long. I deliver to five or six florists each week; I send out my availability list and they tell me what they want.'

Staying on top of one's own garden is often demanding enough as it is, so keeping a high standard across ten gardens requires some careful planning. Sarah explains, 'I used to plant things more like a *garden* garden, but then I realized that it was actually a lot more work for me in terms of weeding, watering, harvesting and just accounting for things.' Sarah's gardens therefore adopt a slightly more 'orderly' appearance, with flowers set out in productive lines, often leaving space to walk between plants. However, as Sarah's gardens show, this doesn't necessarily lead to mono-cropping. 'I plant a lot of different things in the different gardens, which is nice for the owners, but it's also helpful for me. Sometimes I'll have pests such as earwigs or lily beetles in one garden, and in a garden a block away there'll be none.'

Another advantage of growing for local florists and subscribers is the reduction of plant handling and transportation time. Sarah is able to trim, arrange and distribute flowers directly after harvesting them. 'Everything leaves my house within 24 hours of being picked,' she tells me, 'so I'm able to grow many flowers that don't ship well; you can't ship cosmos, foxgloves or zinnias.'

While Sarah takes me around the gardens she pauses intermittently to greet and chat with passers-by, many of whom are local residents. It's clear that Sarah's presence in and out of the Parkdale flower beds is a familiar and valued one for those living in the neighbourhood. As they respond to her with smiles and appreciative comments, it's easy to see how Sarah's small-scale enterprise has benefited many more people than just the garden owners.

THE FLOWER HOUSE

Following the collapse of its principal industry and subsequent filing for bankruptcy in 2013, the once prosperous Motor City of the USA is a very different incarnation of its former landscape. As a result of a rapid fall in the population, many of Detroit's suburban houses were boarded up and left to decay, their interiors becoming time capsules of an era left behind.

It was a pair of such houses that caught the eye of Detroit florist Lisa Waud. Purchasing the properties at auction for just $250, Lisa envisioned a plot of land in which she could cultivate flowers for her Detroit-based cut flower business. Known as 'urban farming', there has been a rise in this kind of property repurposing in one-time affluent cities, such as Detroit. Abandoned and decrepit houses are often worth less than the land on which they're built, resulting in a wider potential for this type of small-scale real estate. Deciding to pay tribute to the former life of one of her newly acquired relics, Lisa delayed its demolition to put together a unique and ambitious project.

The Flower House's exposed rear wall offered the setting for Lisa's own installation. Displaying a mass of hanging delphiniums, her piece was inspired by Dior's Parisian show.

Teams of florists have come from all across the country to participate in this one-off event. Bright dahlias are woven into the fence surrounding the house.

On a chilly Michigan morning in the Detroit suburb of Hamtramck, I meet Lisa on the porch of the recently renamed Flower House. For one weekend only, florists from all over the country have filled the rooms of Lisa's abandoned property with over 36,000 blooms. 'The idea came to me three years ago,' Lisa explains. 'I saw images from the Dior show in Paris, where they constructed really beautiful flower-walls inside a mansion. The whole concept was about nature taking over, and that's what happens here in Detroit in these houses with no one living in them.'

With the event taking place over just three days, the Flower House opens its doors for the first time in over a decade. Visitors to this most temporary of exhibitions are invited to explore the deteriorated rooms, each lovingly adorned with a mass of magnificent flowers. 'To sit empty for 15 years and then have 2,000 people come through in 72 hours places quite a

Lisa Ward (left) sees her vision become a reality as the Flower House opens its doors.

demand on the structural integrity of the house,' Lisa tells me. 'We put a lot of work into making it safe before any of the florists were let loose on the rooms.' This is certainly reassuring to hear when walking around the frail framework of this extraordinarily decorated property. Weaving in and out of the tiny, dilapidated rooms, the enormous wealth of flowers both embellishes and sympathizes with the many household relics that have been left here untouched. For Lisa, the decision to leave these objects in place was an integral element of the project's conception as they tell the story of the house as a home.

In order to make the Flower House a reality, Lisa enlisted the help of her wide network of florists, offering individual teams the opportunity to develop their own floral schemes. 'I feel that if you invite people into a project it's no longer "mine" but "ours",' she explains. 'I love how every

room is different. Take the downstairs bathroom, for example; what they've done is very literal, it's congenial with the setting. And then you come upstairs and there's a tornado of flowers in the dining room.'

With the ground floor room exposed to the elements, the wall itself having collapsed, Lisa's own installation subverts its ramshackle setting with a radiant profusion of blue delphiniums, hung from the ceiling. 'It's fall here right now,' she says, looking up at the house, 'so the natural colours are red, orange and yellow. I really wanted to stay away from those, to not be so seasonal.' It's hard to imagine that this wonderful creation will be pulled down in just two weeks time and the plot returned to soil. But the prospect of its second life is rather an exciting one. 'I'll be growing dahlias and peonies here,' Lisa says, enthusiastically. 'It's going to be a flower farm.'

Sarah's rustic planter is constructed with wood from a local reclamation yard.

FLORAL INFUSIONS

When Sarah Collins decided to renovate the neglected back garden of her family home in Bristol, she saw an opportunity to give it a child-friendly makeover. Surfaced with uneven, cracked paving stones and weed-filled gravel, the somewhat dilapidated garden presented a hazardous environment for her two active young children.

'When we bought the house a few years ago we inherited a backyard that was quite run down,' Sarah says. 'I wanted a fun, safe area for the kids to play in, as well as a bit of a sanctuary for me.' Enlisting the help of friends and family, Sarah cleared away the broken stonework of the garden floor and replaced it with weed-suppressant fabric and a deep layer of bark chip. As she was keen to provide a space in which to grow a few plants, too, Sarah made room for a 2sq. m (21½sq. ft) raised bed. 'Getting the balance right is often hard,' says Sarah. 'Theo and Annie love to run around, and I wanted them to have room to do so. But it was also important to me that there was a designated space for greenery too, somewhere full of life for us all to enjoy.'

Initially intended as a little herb garden, Sarah's raised bed provided somewhere to grow a handful of kitchen essentials, such as chives, marjoram and rosemary. However, as trips to a nearby park began sparking a curiosity in flowers for three-year-old Theo, Sarah decided to extend the use of her compact productive plot and have a go at growing some herself. 'Both of the kids enjoy being around plants,' she says. 'They love all the different shapes and colours; they're forever wanting to pick them!' With such a confined area, Sarah was eager to include flowers offering more than their ornamental value. 'I like plants that can be used in some way or another, as opposed to being simply cosmetic,' she explains. 'I'm a big fan of herbal teas. I'd read somewhere that many garden flowers could be used to make tea, and wanted to give that a try.'

Vivid stems of achillea and astilbe provide herbal and ornamental qualities. However, calendula is Theo's favourite.

As an easy-to-grow herbal favourite, camomile was an obvious choice for Sarah's raised planter. Producing a high yield of bright yellow-and-white flower heads by midsummer, this aromatic herbaceous perennial is often

124

Herbal tea can be made using fresh or dried flower heads. Sarah deadheads her camomile plants, collecting the blooms and storing them in a jar.

quick to establish itself. 'The camomile has already become a bit unruly!' says Sarah, pinching a couple of the little daisy heads from a tall, dainty stem. 'I divided the two original clumps this spring as they'd become too big for the space. I tend to cut the leaves back from time to time now, just to keep them in check.'

When it comes to harvesting her floral crop, the process couldn't be simpler. 'I just pick the flowers as and when they come out,' Sarah says. 'I keep a lock-jar to hand in the kitchen and just drop the heads in whenever I remember to.' As the camomile flowers can be infused with water either dried or freshly picked, a supply of herbal stock can be easily amassed. 'You only really need 2–3 flower heads to make a flavourful mug,' says Sarah.

In addition to camomile, Sarah has made room for several other tea-producing flowers. Large yellow disks of pot marigold (*Calendula officinalis*) are coupled with the tall, nodding heads of *Achillea millefolium*, both of which are believed to contain restorative properties. 'I'm not too experimental with my herbal flowers,' Sarah tells me, 'and they're really only an extension of the flower bed itself. But it is nice to have an active involvement with the plants in our garden; a little connection to the wider natural world.'

1. To make your camomile tea bags you'll need coffee filters, scissors, string, coloured card, a stapler and your dried camomile flowers.

HOW TO: MAKE TEA BAGS WITH YOUR FLOWERS

Growing and harvesting your own herbal teas can be enormously rewarding. Nothing beats a home-grown brew, especially with the convenience of a supply so close to hand. So why not go that extra step and create ready-to-use tea bags from your floral yield? You can also treat them as charming handmade presents for friends.

Of the many plants that offer a delicious herbal infusion, camomile is one of the easiest to grow. The familiar, daisy-shaped flower heads begin forming from late spring and can then be picked and dried to preserve their sweet, meadow-rich flavour. Spread them out on a sheet of paper to dry out or alternatively dry them on the stem, suspended by string in a cool, airy environment.

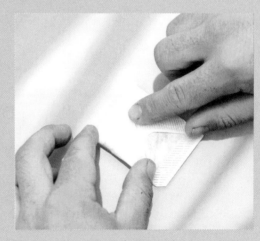

5. Now fold the other side in so that the filter forms a rectangle.

2. Fill a coffee filter with 4–5 dried camomile flowers.

3. Fold the top of the filter down over itself.

4. Fold one side in to make a right angle at the bottom.

6. Cut a 10cm (4in) length of string with a knot at one end.

7. Staple the string to the coffee filter, just above the knot. This will fix the folds in place.

8. Cut a rectangle of coloured card then fold and staple it, forming a tea-bag tab.

Camomile is just one of many flowers with which you can make a flavourful tea. Why not try others? Fennel, calendula and echinacea all offer unique flavour characteristics along with their individual herbal qualities. Available from most garden centres and nurseries, all three are well suited to being grown in pots and containers. It is essential that plants are correctly identified before ingesting them, as well as any potential allergens.

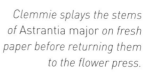

A PRESSING MATTER

When garden space is in short supply or absent altogether, bringing flowers into the home sometimes requires a little creative thinking. For Clemmie Power, a life-long pastime has provided an ornate alternative to a garden of her own.

'I can remember pressing flowers as a child,' says Clemmie. 'My grandparents live in America and I went over there for a family wedding. As a flower girl I was given a bouquet of small white roses and greenery. My grandparents had also given me a flower press, so when I got home I pressed all of my bouquet.' And so began a hobby which has continued into adulthood.

'A friend made me a flower press as a present last year,' says Clemmie. 'It's made from olive ash wood, which is really tough and heavy. The flowers don't stand a chance!' Layered with cardboard dividers, this sturdy implement allows Clemmie to press a large number of flowers at the same time. Typically left to dry out for 3–4 weeks, her flowers are then either stored in notebooks or arranged in picture frames to act as gifts. 'It was only recently that I decided to try out a flower mobile,' says Clemmie. 'I wanted a way to create a more interactive display, something three-dimensional, to get the most out of the pressings.' Lightly strung with sewing thread, Clemmie's flowers are suspended from her hall ceiling, where they make a miniature indoor garden apparently floating below a woven wood wreath.

Yellow freesias and white nigella flowers hang from the woven hazel mobile, suspended in the hallway.

'The idea behind the mobile was to allow light to shine through the flowers,' explains Clemmie. 'Pressed flowers look lovely on paper, but there are intricate details within the petals which are only revealed when they are backlit.' When the delicate floral arrangement is viewed from below, many new elements are exhibited, from complex capillary structures to individual patterns of coloration. And with the flowers weighing so little, they turn on the slightest movement of air, mirroring the natural motion of plants, when caught by the breeze.

Clemmie deliberately kept her display simple. 'It was tempting to add more, but I needed to restrain the arrangement,' she says. 'The mobile looks best with just a handful of flowers; they need to be able to move freely without touching one another.' Refining her pressed palette, Clemmie mixed bright yellow freesias with dusky maroon astrantia. In addition, flattened nigella heads float at the top of the structure, like little moons. For an elegant effect, she used long stems for the mobile so that the flowers would display well, while the base of the mobile was made with twisted hazel stems, woven together to form a circle. 'I used hazel cut from a friend's garden,' says Clemmie. 'They have a wonderful copse which throws up these straight, malleable rods.' Nest-like in its formation, the base offers an ideal framework from which to thread the flowers.

When it comes to the process itself, pressing flowers is not without its challenges. 'It's very much trial and error,' Clemmie says. 'When you open up the press the results can often be disappointing.' Some flowers are unavoidably tricky to press. 'Cornflowers are one of my favourite flowers because of their electric blue. Frustratingly, though, they fade very quickly to a pale pink or white.' Another factor to consider once the flowers have begun pressing is that of moisture; the act of pressing removes liquid from the flowers, and the paper surrounding them soaks it up. Therefore Clemmie must check on her flowers once a week, replacing the paper each time to ensure that they do not become mouldy.

Clemmie's heavy-duty press produces an array of colourful blooms. Those not used for framing or a mobile are decoratively preserved on cartridge paper.

1. Using a handsaw, cut two matching pieces of 10mm (^{2}⁄$_5$in) thick MDF board to 220 x 220mm (8¾ x 8¾in). Alternatively, a timber yard or DIY store may cut them for you. Sand down the edges to a smooth curve.

HOW TO: MAKE YOUR OWN FLOWER PRESS

Beyond the attraction of its natural beauty, a flower can often carry a personal significance that makes it something to treasure in the long term. While a cut flower in a vase will inevitably shrivel and fade, a pressed flower will stand the test of time. With this simple yet traditional press, you can set about retaining both the vibrance of the flower and the sentiment that lies within it.

Once your flowers are pressed, there are various ways to present, catalogue and display them. Collecting them in a notebook with accompanying information such as the date, species and location where they were picked can be a satisfying process. Alternatively, framing flowers as simple single specimens or as a collage can be a rewarding way to preserve and exhibit your pressings.

5. Cut out a rectangle of craft paper that, once folded, has the same dimensions as the cardboard in the previous step. Trim your flowers and attach them to this paper, using thin strips of masking tape.

2. To connect the pieces of MDF you'll need four M8 size bolts with accompanying wing nuts. Using an 8.5mm or 9mm drill bit, drill a hole right through both blocks at each corner.

3. Check the hole alignment by pushing the bolts through both pieces of MDF and fastening the wing nuts.

4. Using a ruler, measure out two identical squares of ordinary cardboard, ensuring that they fit within the margin of the holes. These will act as cushions between the MDF and flowers being pressed.

One of the aims in pressing flowers is to remove moisture from the stem and petals so that they do not rot. As the flowers are squeezed and flattened their moisture is absorbed by the paper, so it is best to replace it once a week to keep it fresh and able to soak up any further dampness.

If you find that there isn't enough room in the flower press for the amount of material you wish to preserve, you can use longer bolts and additional layers of cardboard. The cardboard dividers will prevent flowers being pressed on top of each other, which would lead to markings on the petals.

6. Fold the paper over the flowers and sandwich it between the two squares of card inside the press. The press can now be screwed down tightly. It may be helpful to attach a note detailing the flowers inside.

THE BEE'S NEEDS

Sometimes even the tiniest of garden plots can serve a whole host of different purposes. The process of growing flowers can be an invigorating experience, and the resulting blooms an unparalleled reward. However, the gardeners in this final chapter have sought to create gardens with an additional motivation, offering inventive solutions to a growing concern. With the number of bees now declining on a global scale, the plight of our pollinators is making headline news – and bad news for the bees means bad news for many of our most-loved flowers, not to mention food crops. Even the smallest of domestic gardens now has the opportunity to play a key role in reversing this decline.

BEE FRIENDLY

We've all been there, standing on a monochrome platform, counting down the minutes until our train arrives. However, with the recent arrival of the Bee Friendly Trust's colourful conservation planters, a handful of London's railway stations now offer commuters a productive and engaging way to pass the time.

Set up in 2015 by professional bee keeper Dr Luke Dixon, the Bee Friendly Trust aims to support the dwindling population of honey bees both locally and across the world by raising awareness through planting and educational schemes. 'Putney was our first station,' Dixon tells me. 'The station platforms were looking a little forlorn and we thought planters would brighten up the platforms for commuters while at the same time providing forage for bees.'

Providing year-round forage for bees is at the heart of Dr Luke Dixon's project.

With Putney Station's flower-packed beds proving an enormous success, Dr Dixon's team began extending the reaches of their wildlife-nurturing scheme. Working in conjunction with South West Trains, Bee Friendly erected flower planters further down the tracks. 'We began linking up stations to create pollinator corridors around London,' he says. 'The removal of suitable plants to forage on has been a major factor in the recent decline of the honey bee. Creating corridors of forage has the potential to make a significant contribution to the survival of bees in urban areas.'

Rather uncharacteristically for municipal garden planters, green-fingered commuters are also encouraged to help with their upkeep. 'We want people waiting for their trains to help look after the planters,' says Dr Dixon. With simple tasks, such as deadheading and weeding, commuters can have an active involvement, which in turn offers a sense of shared ownership. 'It really helps with the look of the planters, and we've been delighted with the response. It doesn't always work; some people take the ownership too far and we do have plants stolen. But we also find others planted, so there's a balance.'

Another contributing factor to the planters' success is the plants that have been selected. Those favoured by bees tend to differ a little from the typical plants within council-planned schemes. Dr Dixon explains, 'Honey bees see a different colour spectrum to humans. They don't see red but they do see ultra-violet, and even colours we have no names for. So bees particularly love flowers at the purple and violet end of the spectrum.' Anyone growing lavender on a bright summer's day will certainly testify to this; with flower heads often drooping under the weight of numerous bees, it's a clear favourite. Buddleia, lilac, and rosemary are equally popular.

The frequent use of infertile plants is also a concern for the Bee Friendly Trust. 'So much of our urban ornamental planting is made up of sterile flowers, which are of no use to insects at all,' says Dr Dixon. With this in mind, the Trust has sought to feature some less conventional inclusions that are more likely to be found adorning a wild hedgerow or hillside than a city planter. Standing by one of Putney station's flower beds, I notice a clump of pink thrift (*Armeria maritima*), its bright, clustered flowers pushing up through the compost. I can't resist the urge to deadhead the dulled, finished stems as I would in my own garden. It feels both wonderfully satisfying and yet strangely against the rules.

Nectar-rich flowers have been selected for use in the station planters. Key plants include geranium (top left), foxglove (far right) and allium (bottom left).

We hope you enjoy the flowers.
Please help:
DEADHEAD
WEED
DONATE

bee friendly trust

Alan's truck sits proudly at the entrance to Cleeve Nursery on the outskirts of Bristol.

TRUCK STOP

'**People are astounded,**' nurseryman Alan Down says enthusiastically, '**they get their phones out straight away.**' Walking me around his four-wheeled flower bed, he describes the reactions from people encountering his 'pickup pollinator' for the first time. '**They just love to see fun in the garden. Hopefully they also come away with the message that we have an opportunity to do much more for bees in our own gardens.**'

Originally conceived as an eye-catching and educational display for the Chelsea Fringe Festival, Alan's truck garden now adorns the entrance to his plant nursery on the outskirts of Bristol. Held in conjunction with the RHS Chelsea Flower Show in London, the Chelsea Fringe celebrates the alternative side of gardening. 'I was actually looking to plant up an old Morris Minor for the festival, or an Indian rickshaw!' Alan says. With the high demand for repurposing these kinds of vehicle, he decided instead to go with a pickup truck on offer at a local scrap metal dealer: 'Strangely, he'd had the same idea, so he helped to remove the engine and strip down the pickup.'

Blue aster (Felicia amelloides 'Santa Anita'), white argyranthemum and yellow monkey flower (Mimulus guttatus) produce a dense mat of flowers within the pickup planting.

The truck provides a range of planting environments, from deep soil in the pickup bed to arid conditions below the bonnet.

Alan believes that there's an opportunity for residential gardens to significantly bolster the number of bees.

Tall spires of globe thistle (far left) rise above Alan's pickup – a plant almost as irresistible to bees as Salvia nemorosa *(below left).*

With flowers spilling abundantly from every feature of the truck, there's a wonderful sense of playfulness. Beneath the raised bonnet spring wallflowers and chives; sacks of bedding plants are suspended along the chassis, and there's even a scarecrow at the wheel. However, behind the lively, whimsical nature of Alan's Pickup Pollinator there's a message that lies very close to his heart. 'With the rise in monoculture farming and the consequential lack of wild flowers, the countryside is becoming ever more commercialized,' he tells me. 'I have sympathy with the farmers. They're being squeezed by low prices and a global food market, and are therefore having to be as efficient as possible; but there's less and less room for wildlife.'

On a more positive note, Alan has also noticed a shift in the type of plants that now interest residential gardeners. With bee- and butterfly-friendly plants becoming increasingly popular, he's seen a definite move towards a more supportive interaction with nature. 'As a plant nursery we have a role to play in encouraging people to provide for wildlife in their own gardens,' he says. 'As bees are coming under threat, we're trying to promote our message as much as we can.'

Combining his nurseryman's knowledge and enthusiasm for wildlife, Alan has designed his pickup-planting around attracting the greatest volume of insects and pollinators possible. Comprising annuals, perennials, shrubs and bulbs, the little truck garden offers a wide and varied source of nectar-rich flowers. From the clustered whites of *Cotoneaster salicifolius* to the tall purple spires of *Salvia nemorosa*, bees and hoverflies are drawn in by a magnificent array of colour. 'What we've tried to do is to have successional flowers,' Alan explains. 'The early bees that emerge after winter need just as much pollen and nectar as those which come out in summer.' Therefore, by providing a steady flow of sequential blooms, the pickup can offer a food supply for the majority of the year.

Lifting the thick foliage at the back of the truck, Alan points out an alpine strawberry. 'Those have been pollinated by the bees,' he says. 'There's a huge amount of variety here. As soon as a gap appears we'll put something new in.' The pickup pollinator also offers a variety of growing conditions. With the bonnet raised and obstructing rainfall, the engine section is particularly dry, dictating the kinds of plants used. *Sedum spectabile*, chive alliums and wallflowers all thrive in this less irrigated environment. Conversely, the back of the truck is filled with approximately 45cm (18in) of soil, providing a much deeper and more saturated growing medium. Almost bursting at the seams, this section contributes some of the damp-favouring meadow species such as comfrey, nasturtium and the Spanish daisy, *Erigeron karvinskianus*. The cab of the pickup truck even acts as a miniature greenhouse, a climate Alan has made the most of with the inclusion of tomato plants; not an inch of his truck has been wasted in his search to help the bees.

ROOFTOP WETLAND

There can't be many people as well versed in constructing peculiarly placed gardens as Dusty Gedge. As a green infrastructure consultant, Dusty's speciality is roof gardens, and with an impressive high-rise record he's never shied away from a new challenge.

Invited to consider the ageing roof of one of central London's most cherished museums, Dusty stumbled upon an opportunity to experiment with an idea he had long been wanting to try. Guiding me along a walkway at the top of London's Victoria and Albert Museum, he says, 'I found a series of roofs each encompassing two slopes leading down to a flat surface. Rain water running off the slopes collects in a central gully, which is about 15cm (6in) deep. By damming the run-off exit, I could have rain water sitting in that gully, replicating a wetland environment.'

Hidden within the enormous expanse of the V&A's rooftop, Dusty's wetland occupies an area of about 8sq. m (86sq. ft), forming the most unexpected oasis one could imagine. Rounding the right-hand slope, I'm met with a familiar host of flowers in the most unfamiliar setting. Riverside regulars, such as purple loosestrife (*Lythrum salicaria*), ragged robin (*Lychnis flos-cuculi*), and water forget-me-not (*Myosotis scorpioides*) weave among sedge grass and pebbles. There are damp-loving species, such as cuckoo flower (*Cardamine pratensis*) and water mint (*Mentha aquatica*), which one might encounter along the fringes of a natural pond. The planting is so lush that it takes a moment before the water is visible, reflecting the ox-eye daisies (*Leucanthemum vulgare*) and buttercups (*Ranunculus acris*).

Dusty's wetland has
created a resource
for the V&A's
beehives (left).

'I had always wanted to make a wetland roof for nature,' Dusty tells me, stepping carefully through the dense planting. 'Most of my roofs are dry grassland, so this was a completely different situation.' And 'different' is certainly the word. I ask Dusty how he set about orchestrating such a precarious and adventurous project; surely the potential of an overflowing roof was a little unnerving? 'When it rains the garden takes on a lot of water,' he says. 'If it leaked it wasn't going to leak into a house, it was going to leak onto very, very precious objects.' Bringing in an experienced green roof contractor, Active Ecology, Dusty's team set about designing and constructing a system that would make sure the museum remained safe and dry. 'Once the water level reaches a certain depth it triggers a weir, which then lets excess water out into the drain.' In this way, harvested rainwater is repurposed as a resource for nature, while at the same time never accumulating to the extent of posing a risk to the roof.

As president of the EFB (European Federation of Green Roof Associations), Dusty has placed nature at the very heart of his waterlogged creation, making the V&A's wetland garden the epitome of successful green infrastructure. Bumble bees, dragonflies, hoverflies and even water snails have all found their way up onto the roof, the last of which came as an additional surprise. 'They just turned up!' exclaims Dusty. 'The nearest pond is probably in Kensington Gardens. One theory is that they were brought here on the feet of a visiting heron.' The garden has provided a refuge for a wide range of creatures, like a kind of high-rise watering hole for transitory wildlife. 'The idea was that it would become self-maintained,' says Dusty. 'I like seeing a few dead stems. Solitary bees will very often over-winter in tall ones, so we'll try to leave them at least until April or May when the bees are likely to have left.'

Alongside its influx of natural newcomers, the wetland planting also serves the museum's resident bee hives, which is how V&A volunteer Rena Melnyczuk came to be engaged with the garden. 'As a gardener I kept looking at it and thinking "I'm not sure that looks right!"' she tells me. 'In my own garden there are lots of things I would have pulled up by that time. I hadn't fully appreciated that it just had to grow naturally.' It didn't take long before Rena's interpretation of the space began to shift. Seeing the space develop, she soon fell in love with it. 'It's very peaceful. At about 11 o'clock in the morning, with no one else up here, it's something very special. I've ended up planting a lot of the same plants in my own garden now!'

'We're trying to demonstrate that you don't have to make roof gardens formal – you can make natural prairies,' says Dusty. 'This roof told us what we could do. The garden has been designed to fit this situation; we haven't imposed anything on it, which I think is kind of cool.'

ELEVATED AROMA

Where growing space really is in short supply, choosing the right flowers can be a tough decision, for when they fill what little room is available the selected plants are required to offer far more than just their summer blooms. Dressing the window of her rooftop apartment in Paris, Lucy Davies was faced with just this dilemma.

'I think everybody starts out with high expectations for their window boxes,' Lucy says with a smile. 'There's so much pressure on that one small plot, especially when it's the only bit of garden you have!' With its narrow yet sun-soaked window ledge, Lucy's modest but stylish apartment sits at the top of a residential block in the heart of the French capital. Like many inner-city apartments of its kind, it has a wooden-clad window railing and this provides the support for Lucy's hanging planter. 'I wanted something simple for that confined space, elegant yet versatile,' she explains. 'It can be wonderful just putting one kind of plant on a site and watching it do its thing.'

It wasn't until a trip to Pas de Calais in Northern France that Lucy found the inspiration for her compact little window garden. 'I was visiting a friend along the coast and encountered the most spectacular lavender shrubs I'd ever seen. It was an unseasonably warm, early summer evening and the scent of the flowers was just incredible.' Enchanted with the sheer mass of delicate blue flowers and their intoxicating aroma, Lucy was drawn to the striking shrubs. However, there was an additional element which affirmed that lavender was the plant for Lucy. 'I couldn't believe how many bees there were,' she says. 'The flower heads were smothered in them, which really brought the plants to life'. Passionate about nature and the importance of bees, Lucy was excited to bring a little of this rural spectacle into her high-rise home.

Bearing a profusion of scented flower heads, Lavandula angustifolia 'Grosso' makes for an ideal balcony bouquet.

Positioned in full sun and lined with hessian, Lucy's planter provides the kind of conditions that lavender tends to thrive in. 'I'm amazed how happy the plants have been,' says Lucy. 'I read that although lavender requires regular watering, it hates sitting in damp soil, so the hessian is there to help prevent the roots from becoming saturated.' Opting for one of the more reliable, showy forms, Lucy picked out *Lavandula angustifolia* 'Grosso' at a local garden centre. 'This variety was apparently grown for its particularly long stems and strong scent, so it was perfect for the apartment,' she says. 'I bought two of them; it's amazing how quickly they've filled the container.'

When it comes to the provision of nectar for foraging city bees, lavender flowers perform a crucial role. With a natural slump in available garden blooms between June and July, they fill the gap at a critical time for developing hives. Says Lucy, 'Honey being produced here by urban bee keepers is of just as high a standard as in the countryside. So it's great to be growing a plant which in a small way contributes forage for some of Paris's bees.' By pruning back the spent flowers in one cut each year, the plants can be kept compact, leaving their silvery foliage as interest throughout the winter. The by-product of this is the resulting bounty of aromatic cut stems. 'I keep all of the cuttings and hang them in bunches to dry out,' says Lucy. 'It's wonderful to cook with, and occasionally I make small aromatic pouches, either to go under the pillow or as gifts for friends.'

At the end of the summer, once the bees have had their fill, Lucy cuts back the stems and ties them into bunches.

HOW TO: MAKE A LAVENDER BAG

Typically, lavender is pruned back once a year, leaving you with a bounty of fresh, heavily scented stems that can be put to many different uses. For example, they can be pressed to release a fragrant oil, made into tea and even rubbed on the skin as an insect repellent. Probably the most rewarding way to take advantage of a plant with such a long-lasting aroma, though, is to make a lavender bag. Hung with clothes, nestled in the sock drawer or even placed under your pillow, it is a great way to bring the freshness of the summer into your home.

1. You will need hessian fabric, scissors, a ruler, a pen, a large needle, thick thread, ribbon and lavender prunings.

2. Taking your hessian and ruler, measure out and cut a rectangle sized 15 x 20cm (6 x 8in). Draw a line exactly down the centre with a marker pen.

3. Fold the hessian rectangle in half. Sew together the long edge and one of the two shorter edges. This will leave you with a pouch which is open at the top.

4. Turn the hessian pouch inside out, then fill it nearly to the top with your dried lavender heads, removed from their stalks.

5. Holding the bag at the top, pinch in the sides and tie tightly with ribbon.

SOURCES

USEFUL WEBSITES

Portia Baker
Landscape architect based in Richmond, Surrey
www.portiabaker.com

Janet Boulton
More information on Janet's work can be found at
www.janetboulton.co.uk

Hoopla Garden
www.theediblebusstop.org

Garden Museum
www.gardenmuseum.org.uk

No.21 Flowers
Alex Hales' Boutique florist in Aberystwyth, Wales:
www.no21flowers.co.uk

My Luscious Backyard
Based in Toronto, Canada, Sarah Nixon provides seasonal,
sustainable cut flowers. For more information visit her website:
www.mylusciousbackyard.ca

Flower House
www.theflower.house

Bee Friendly
The wonderful work of the Bee Friendly Trust is documented
on their website: www.beefriendlytrust.org

Cleeve Nursery
www.cleevenursery.co.uk

Dusty Gedge
Dusty's blog details the many interesting projects he has
been engaged in: www.dustygedge.co.uk

Dutch Bulbs
Bulbs for the author's 'Pottering Around' feature were supplied
by J. Parker's. Their enormous range of plants and bulbs can be
viewed at www.jparkers.co.uk
For the J. Parker's wholesale range, visit www.dutchbulbs.co.uk

AUTHORS

WORDS BY
MATT COLLINS

Matt Collins came to writing from a horticultural background. He trained at the National Botanic Garden of Wales before taking up a consultancy position with the Garden Museum in London and serving as head gardener for a private residence in Richmond. Passionate about wild flowers, he is interested in the intersection of city and natural landscapes, and the ways in which naturalized flora responds to manmade environments. Matt documents his written and horticultural work at orangetip.co.uk.

PHOTOGRAPHY BY
ROO LEWIS

Roo Lewis is a fashion and advertising photographer based from his North London studio. Growing up in Dorset he was surrounded by the natural world and now chooses to base much of his personal work on exploring the subject. When not shooting for clients such as VICE, Getty, Topshop, Audi and Sony, Roo can be found in the darkroom printing his latest projects. www.roolewis.com

I would like to thank everyone at Pavilion involved in putting this book together; in particular Katie, Diana, Laura and Claire. Special thanks to Krissy for managing the book's development and for her dependable guidance, planning and support throughout.

This book wouldn't have been possible without Roo Lewis' beautiful photography. His efforts to capture flowering plants during an abnormally damp and overcast summer are testament to the great level of skill with which he operates. Roo's persistent willingness to free up time for last-minute jaunts up and down the country have also contributed immensely to the realization of *My Tiny Flower Garden*.

I am enormously grateful to each of the gardeners who have shared their unique and wonderful green spaces with us. It's been a great experience visiting the gardens and documenting something of the stories behind their creation. Many thanks also to Alice and Ady for the loan of their gorgeous flat, in which we shot some of the book's practical features.

Lastly I want to thank Clementine for her immeasurable support over this last year. Aside from her unceasing patience with my frequent flower trips both at home and abroad, much of this book is owed to her continued input, advice and encouragement.